# Working with Parents of Children with Special Educational Needs

# About the authors

Chris Dukes is a qualified teacher with over 20 years' experience. She has worked in various London primary schools as a class teacher and later as a member of the Senior Management Team. Chris has a Masters degree in Special Needs and through her later role as a SENCO and support teacher, many years' experience of working with children with a variety of needs. Chris has worked closely with staff teams, mentoring, advising and supervising work with children with additional needs, as well as with other education and health professionals. Chris currently works as an Area SENCO supporting Special Needs Coordinators and managers in a wide range of pre-school settings. As well as advising she writes courses, delivers training and produces publications.

Maggie Smith began her career as a nursery teacher in Birmingham. She has worked as a peripatetic teacher for an under-5s EAL Team and went on to become the Foundation Stage manager of an Early Years Unit in Inner London. Maggie helped to set up an innovative unit for young children with behavioural difficulties and has also worked supporting families of children with special needs. She has taught on Early Years BTEC and CACHE courses at a college of higher education. She currently works as an Area SENCO supporting Special Needs Co-ordinators and managers in a wide range of pre-school settings. As well as advising she writes courses, delivers training and produces publications.

# Working with Parents of Children with Special Educational Needs

Chris Dukes and Maggie Smith

Illustrations by Simon Smith

P·C·P

Paul Chapman
Publishing

Paul Chapman Publishing
A SAGE Publications Company
1 Oliver's Yard
55 City Road
London EC1Y 1SP

Sage Publications Inc
2455 Teller Road
Thousand Oaks, California 91320

SAGE Publications India Pvt Ltd
B 1/I1 Mohan Cooperative Industrial Area
Mathara Road
New Delhi 110 044

SAGE Publications Asia – Pacific Pte Ltd
33 Pekin Street #02-01
Far East Street
Singapore 048763

**Library of Congress Control Number: 2007934407**

**British Library Cataloguing in Publication Data**
A catalogue record for this book is available from the British Library

ISBN 978-1-4129-4521-9
ISBN 978-1-4129-4522-6 (pbk)

Typeset by Pantek Arts Ltd, Maidstone, Kent
Printed in Great Britain by Cromwell Press Ltd, Trowbridge, Wiltshire
Printed on paper from sustainable forests

# Contents

# Contents of the CD-ROM

## How to use the CD-ROM

The CD-ROM contains pdf files, labelled 'Worksheets.pdf', which contain worksheets from this book. You will need Acrobat Reader version 3 or higher to view and print these pages.

The document is set to print at A4 but you can enlarge them to A3 by increasing the output percentage using the page set-up settings for your printer.

Throughout the book, you will see this CD icon used. This indicates that the material you are looking at is also available electronically on the accompanying CD-ROM.

## Contents of the CD-ROM

01. Working with Parents Quiz
02. Working in Partnership with Parents Action Plan pro-forma
03. Starter Ideas: 20 Easy Ways to Support Good Relations with *All* Parents
04. Emotions Parents May Go Through
05. Good Listening Skills
06. Open Questions to Use with Parents
07. Questions to Consider for My Audit and Action Plan
08. Audit and Action Plan: *Information* about a Child's Needs pro-forma
09. Audit and Action Plan: *Skills* Needed to Meet a Child's Needs pro-forma
10. Sample Audit and Action Plan: *Information* about a Child's Needs
11. Sample Audit and Action Plan: *Skills* Needed to Meet a Child's Needs
12. 20 Ways to Recognise an Inclusive Setting
13. Sample Inclusion Policy
14. More About Me information pro-forma
15. Top Tips for Staff Who Carry Out Home Visits
16. Home Visit Sample Letter of Introduction
17. Let's Talk About ...Working Together to Settle Your Child into Pre-school
18. Ideas for Improving Transitions
19. Factors to Consider When Working with Parents and Families
20. Maintaining Professionalism and Knowing Your Boundaries
21. Sharing Skills
22. Sample Individual Education Plan
23. Let's Talk About ... Individual Plans or Individual Education Plans
24. Communicating with Parents
25. 10 Tips for Preparing for Meetings with Parents
26. 10 Tips for Meetings with Parents
27. Sample Letter of Invitation
28. Meeting Prompt Sheet for Parents pro-forma

# Acknowledgements

This book is dedicated to our parents, who have helped to make us the people we are today.

For Iris Dukes: with much love and thanks for 'being there'.

In loving memory of Roy Dukes and Margaret and Edward Smith, who we know would be proud of this book.

# Introduction

*Every child in my class leaves someone to come to school each day and each child returns to someone. I will fully know and teach that child only when I connect with that someone.*
(Hurt, 2000: 88)

The aim of this book is to support practitioners to work in partnership with parents, particularly those parents who have children with special or additional needs.

The benefits of working closely with parents are many. In our experience practitioners recognise this – they want the best for the children they work with and aspire to build positive relationships with the children's parents or carers.

There is, however, little practical guidance about the day-to-day activities, policies and procedures that pre-schools can employ to help support those relationships. There is even less advice for practitioners on ways to think and reflect upon their own personal skills and attitudes. In this guide we provide the hands-on practical guidance which practitioners have been asking for.

We hope that as more children with special or additional needs are welcomed and included in their local pre-schools and nurseries, practitioners will find the ideas and activities in this book invaluable.

In writing this book we have set out to:

▶ promote the benefits of working with parents for practitioner, parent and child

▶ help practitioners reflect on and develop their own personal skills

▶ give practical guidance, tips, leaflets and pro-formas which can be used in practitioners' everyday work

▶ signpost both parents and practitioners to available support and advice.

## Pre-school practitioners

The book will guide you through the legislation and government recommendations on working with parents, provide you with the tools to start developing your own personal skills and suggest ways to involve and communicate better with parents. Sample letters and other pro-formas, both photcopiable and on the CD-Rom, can be used as suggested in the book or personalised to suit your own setting.

The hands-on activities will provide starting points for team discussion.

## Tutors and students

This book discusses some of the issues surrounding working effectively with parents. It gives sound guidance about how pre-schools can improve their practice in this area and lay strong foundations for working in partnership.

## Advisers

Use this book to support pre-schools in building better working relationships with parents. Individual chapters, hands-on activities and case studies can be used as the basis for training or staff development.

## A note on the text

The case studies in this publication are a composite of numerous children and families in various settings, compiled over the authors' many years of experience, and are not specific to any one child, parent, practitioner or setting.

## CHAPTER ONE

# A solid foundation: basic principles of why and how

The aim of this chapter is to illustrate the importance of practitioners working in partnership with parents. It explores the principles which underpin this relationship and outlines relevant documents. It gives practitioners the opportunity to consider how they work with parents in their own setting.

The chapter sets out:

◗ A parent's perspective

◗ Government guidance and recommendations

◗ A starter quiz – 'Working with Parents'

It also offers hands-on activities.

# Welcome to Holland

I am often asked to describe the experience of raising a child with a disability – to try to help people who have not shared that unique experience to understand it, to imagine how it would feel. It's like this …

When you're going to have a baby, it's like planning a fabulous vacation trip – to Italy. You buy a bunch of guide books and make your wonderful plans. The Coliseum. The Michelangelo David. The gondolas in Venice. You may learn some handy phrases in Italian. It's all very exciting.

After months of eager anticipation, the day finally arrives. You pack your bags and off you go. Several hours later, the plane lands. The stewardess comes in and says, 'Welcome to Holland'.

'<u>Holland</u>?!?' you say. 'What do you mean Holland?? I signed up for Italy! I'm supposed to be in Italy. All my life I've dreamed of going to Italy.'

But there's been a change in the flight plan. They've landed in Holland and there you must stay.

The important thing is that they haven't taken you to a horrible, disgusting, filthy place, full of pestilence, famine and disease. It's just a different place.

So you must go out and buy new guide books. And you must learn a whole new language. And you will meet a whole new group of people you would never have met.

It's just a <u>different</u> place. It's slower-paced than Italy, less flashy than Italy. But after you've been there for a while and you catch your breath, you look around … and you begin to notice that Holland has windmills … and Holland has tulips. Holland even has Rembrandts.

But everyone you know is busy coming and going from Italy … and they're all bragging about what a wonderful time they had there. And for the rest of your life, you will say 'Yes, that's where I was supposed to go. That's what I had planned'.

And the pain of that will never, ever, ever, *ever* go away … because the loss of that dream is a very very significant loss.

But … if you spend your life mourning the fact that you didn't get to Italy, you may never be free to enjoy the very special, the very lovely things … about Holland

## Our starting point

Emily Perl Kingsley wrote her poem 'Welcome to Holland' in 1987 after the birth of her own child. For us, when writing this guide, it seemed a good place to begin as it helps to illustrate how the parents of a child with special or additional needs *may* be feeling – we emphasise *may* as, like all individuals, each parent is unique and some may feel differently.

However, we know that through meeting and working with many parents over the years Emily's poem has helped *us* to gain insight into what it means to be the mother or father of a child with special or additional needs and, further, that it has helped *us* to begin to understand the special value of parenting such a child.

## Why work with parents?

For the parents of a child with an additional or special need the path to pre-school has been at best bumpy, at worst a series of hospital stays, appointments and meetings with a whole host of professionals, often retelling their story over and over again. Most parents have embarked upon a long road to understanding their child's condition and how best to meet their own child's needs. Practitioners need to know how to best tap into this wealth of knowledge that parents have and recognise that for parents to leave their precious, often vulnerable child at pre-school is a hard step. Parents need to be able to trust practitioners and feel assured that they, as parents, will be allowed to be involved and consulted as their child progresses through the pre-school years.

Over ten years ago, another parent, Cory Moore, when speaking to professionals, said:

*We need respect; we need to have our contribution valued. We need to participate, not merely be involved. It is, after all, the parent who knew the child first and who knows the child best. Our relationship with our sons and daughters is personal and spans a lifetime.* (Moore, 1993: 49)

Early years Practitioners already recognise the importance of working in partnership with *all* parents and often go the extra mile to ensure parents are involved in every aspect of their child's care and education. The best learning takes place for children when practitioner and parent are working together.

Through this guide we will illustrate how best practice can be achieved by all practitioners for the benefit of those most important to us all, the young child.

## Guidance and recommendations

The government has made it policy over the past few years to create good quality, affordable childcare and education for all children.

At the heart of this policy lies *Every Child Matters*, a document which identifies five outcomes for children that should be achieved no matter where they live, whatever their needs or the services they use.

The outcomes are that children should be helped to:

▶ be healthy

▶ stay safe

▶ enjoy and achieve

▶ make a positive contribution

▶ achieve economic well-being.

The government's ten-year strategy for childcare, *Choice for Parents, the Best Start for Children*, promised to establish a single coherent development and learning framework for all young children from birth to the age of five.

From September 2008 the **Early Years Foundation Stage (EYFS)** is the relevant framework and plays an important role in helping children achieve all five of the *Every Child Matters* outcomes.

Like all government guidance and recommendations it has a strong emphasis on working in partnership with parents, especially those parents who have children with special or additional needs.

The principles of the EYFS are grouped into four distinct but complementary themes:

▶ A unique child

▶ Positive relationships

▶ Enabling environments

▶ Learning and development

The themes of 'A unique child' and 'Positive relationships' in particular highlight the importance of celebrating diversity, inclusion and partnership with parents.

Guidance as to how these principles can be put into everyday practice is described on the 'Principles into Practice' cards which accompany the framework.

**EYFS: THEMES AND COMMITMENTS**

**A Unique Child**

*Card 1.2  Inclusive Practice*

*The diversity of individuals and communities is valued and respected. No child or family is discriminated against.*

**Positive Relationships**

*Card 2.2  Parents as Partners*

*Parents are children's first and most enduring educators. When parents and practitioners work together in early years settings, the results have a positive impact on children's development and learning.*

The statutory guidance also describes how the EYFS sets out to create equality of opportunity and a framework for partnership working which it identifies as underpinning the successful delivery of the EYFS.

**On working in partnership with parents**

*Close-working between early years practitioners and parents is vital for the identification of children's learning needs and to ensure a quick response to any area of particular difficulty.*

*Parents and families are central to a child's wellbeing and practitioners should support this important relationship by sharing information and offering support to learning in the home.*

**On working in partnership with others**

*Practitioners will frequently need to work with professionals from other agencies such as local and community health services, or where children are looked after by the Local Authority, to identify and meet needs and use their knowledge and advice to provide children's social care with the best learning opportunities and environments for all children.*

**On providing for equality of opportunity**

*Providers have a responsibility to ensure positive attitudes to diversity and difference – not only so that every child is included and not disadvantaged, but also so that they learn from the earliest age to value diversity in others and grow up making a positive contribution to society.*

All government guidance and recommendations, including the EYFS, also have a strong emphasis on working in partnership with parents, especially those parents who have children with special or additional needs.

Other bodies concerned with the quality of childcare and education such as **Ofsted** also place importance on the relationship between professionals and parents.

Under the Ofsted framework of inspection, inspectors are required to assess the contribution that parents make to the pre-school and the children's learning. They also evaluate the effectiveness of the links with parents, the quality of the links with the community and the links with other early years settings and providers.

Some legislation which is more specific to children with special or additional needs and their parents, such as the Special Educational Needs Code of Practice (2001), also stresses the need and benefit of practitioner and parent working together in the best interests of the child.

The Code of Practice dedicates a whole chapter to working in partnership and outlines certain expectations with regard to all stages of a child's education. These begin in the early years and pre-school practitioners and settings are expected to 'have regard' to them.

These expectations include a series of principles that preschool settings are expected to adhere to, as well references to policies and procedures.

## The principles of the Code of Practice:

> Every child with special educational needs should have their needs met.

> As far as possible these needs will be met within a mainstream setting with access to a broad, balanced and relevant curriculum.

> The views of parents should be sought and taken into account.

> Wherever possible the views of the child should be taken into account.

(DFEE, 2001: 2:2, p. 16)

One of the key principles of the Special Educational Needs Code of Practice therefore is the importance of working in partnership with parents.

*Parents hold key information and have a crucial role to play in their children's education. They have unique strengths, knowledge and experience to contribute to the shared view of a child's needs and the best way of supporting them. It is therefore essential that all professionals actively seek to work with parents and value the contribution they make.*

*The work of professionals can be more effective when parents are involved and account taken of their wishes, feelings and perspectives on their child's development. This is particularly so when a child has special educational needs.*

*All parents of children with special educational needs should be treated as partners.*

## Hands-on activity

Use the 'Working with Parents Quiz' to help you measure how well you are working with the parents in your setting.

Look carefully at your score and put together an action plan to make improvements (see the template provided on page 10).

Whatever your score on the 'Working with Parents' starter quiz you will find the Starter Ideas on page 11 a useful basis for improving your working partnership with *all* parents.

These starter ideas are expanded further to illustrate how they can be used more specifically when building relationships with those parents of children with special or additional needs.

# Working with Parents Quiz

1. Have you recently surveyed parents' views on any aspect of your setting?
   - (a) Yes
   - (b) Not recently
   - (c) No

2. Do all staff recognise the importance of working with parents?
   - (a) Yes
   - (b) Some
   - (c) No

3. Do you communicate with parents in a range of different ways, e.g. through a newsletter, notice board, etc.?
   - (a) Yes
   - (b) Sometimes but could do more
   - (c) No

4. Do you regularly offer information about your planning and the curriculum?
   - (a) Yes
   - (b) Sometimes
   - (c) No

5. Do you involve parents in their children's learning?
   - (a) Yes
   - (b) Sometimes
   - (c) No

6. Is your pre-school environment physically accessible to all parents?
   - (a) Yes
   - (b) Parts of it
   - (c) No

7. Do parents have the chance to meet with staff regularly to discuss their child?
   - (a) Yes
   - (b) Not regularly
   - (c) No

8. Do you have systems in place to allow parents to contribute their views and opinions?
   - (a) Yes
   - (b) Some but need more
   - (c) No

9. Do parents take a part in the wider life of the pre-school, e.g. by volunteering etc.?
   (a) Yes
   (b) Sometimes
   (c) No

10. Are you aware of local and national parent support organisations, e.g. Parents for Inclusion?
    (a) Yes
    (b) Some but could investigate more
    (c) No

11. Do you hold an annual parent/child event?
    (a) Yes
    (b) Sometimes
    (c) No

12. Do you have a parent space for parents waiting, meeting or settling their children?
    (a) Yes
    (b) Thinking about creating one
    (c) No

## Scoring

For each answer (a) score 3 points; answer (b) score 2 points; answer (c) score 1 point.

Score between 28 and 36

* **Gold Star** awarded – you are well on your way to working successfully with parents. This book will help you go the extra mile.

Score between 20 and 27

* **Silver Star** awarded – you are half way there! Well done. This book will help you clarify your ideas and improve even further.

Score between 12 and 19

* **Bronze Star** awarded – you still have quite a long way to go. *However*, you have made a good start by consulting this book. We are sure you will find the following ideas and suggestions helpful. Go for it!

# Working in Partnership with Parents Action Plan

| Area to be improved | How this is to be achieved (including person/s responsible) | By when | Cost and resources | Evaluation |
|---|---|---|---|---|
| | | | | |

Working with Parents of Children with Special Educational Needs, Paul Chapman Publishing © Chris Dukes and Maggie Smith, 2007

## Starter Ideas: 20 Easy Ways to Support Good Relations with *All* Parents

1.  Make a list of parents' names and use them regularly.

2.  Greet all parents and children every day.

3.  Celebrate birthdays and special days for families and children.

4.  Involve parents as volunteers and fundraisers.

5.  Have a conversation at least weekly with every parent about their child (keep an informal list).

6.  Listen carefully to what parents have to say about their child. Acknowledge they know best.

7.  Share positive events of the day through talk, or send home notes or photographs.

8.  Keep parents informed about bumps and scrapes.

9.  Make sure parents know what is happening in the setting – use a newsletter and have a notice board.

10. Keep a register of parents' skills; ask them how they think they can support the pre-school.

11. Ask parents to contribute to record-keeping.

12. Establish a pattern of talking to parents about everyday matters. This will make it easier to discuss difficult issues.

13. Deal with issues and difficulties the same day as they occur.

14. Remind parents about agreements, payments, etc. in a way that is non-embarrassing.

15. Support parents to get to know each other by introductions, coffee mornings, socials, etc.

16. Tell parents who their child is friendly with and encourage play dates.

17. Encourage parents to tell you social stories about their child.

18. Set up a small comfortable 'Parents' Space' for parents waiting or settling their children.

19. Hold an annual parent/child event such as a concert or a picnic.

20. Have a notice board for parents' use only.

# How the Starter ideas relate to the parents of children with SEN/additional needs

1. **Make a list of parents' names and use them regularly**

   As a key worker or as the setting manager or SENCO, you will build a close relationship with the parents of a child with special/additional needs. It is vital then that you start on a good footing. Find out their name, ask them what they would like you to call them and decide what you would like to be called in return. Make time for regular contact with these parents – this can be face to face, over the telephone or by using a daily home/school diary.

2. **Greet all parents and children every day**

   Make sure you talk to whoever brings any child with special/additional needs to school. Important information may need to be given to you about medication, appointments or how a child has slept.

3. **Celebrate birthdays and special days for families and children**

   Children with special/additional needs may, through circumstance, have less contact with other families. It is important then to make the most of any opportunity such as birthdays or other special days to raise the child's profile within your setting. Involve the child's parents in any planned celebrations.

4. **Involve parents as volunteers and fundraisers**

   Many parents of children with special/additional needs do not go to work outside the home so are often available to get involved in fundraising activities within the preschool. Also many families of children with special/additional needs may already have links with charitable organisations and groups. Consider whether your setting may be able to hold fundraising events such as a jumble sale or a sponsored event on behalf of the group. This will go a long way to ensure good relations with parents as they see the pre-school staff making such efforts on behalf of their child and others.

5. **Have a conversation at least weekly with every parent about their child (keep an informal list)**

   As well as a daily chat with parents it is worth trying to set aside a short time weekly or every two weeks to talk to the parents of any child with special/additional needs. This more formal meeting gives an opportunity to share information and deal with any issues that may arise. This meeting can be held with the SENCO or key worker.

6. **Listen carefully to what parents have to say about their child. Acknowledge they know best**

   Make sure that during any meetings you are listening closely to parents. Make sure conversations take place in a quiet area with little disturbance (this is difficult in many pre-schools). Read and familiarise yourself with the listening skills described in Chapter 2 'The toolkit'.

7. **Share positive events of the day through talk, or send home notes or photographs**

   During daily talks with parents make sure you start any conversation with a positive. If there is a digital camera available, photograph the child carrying out activities or playing with a friend. Share the photographs with parents and regularly print them to be sent home.

8. **Keep parents informed about bumps and scrapes**

   When a child has special/additional needs it is particularly important to inform parents of any mishaps that have occurred within the setting. The smallest bump or scratch could affect some children, e.g. those with a low immune system. Some children may not be able to explain to their parents later, perhaps at bath time, how they came to have a bump or scratch. Parents will always appreciate being kept informed.

9. **Make sure parents know what is happening in the setting – use a newsletter and have a notice board.**

   Pre-empting and informing parents of children with special/additional needs of any proposed or planned occurences such as changes in routines or planned visits outside the pre-school is often a good idea. Planning for change is very important for some children, e.g. those with an autistic spectrum disorder, and practitioner and parents need to work closely to avoid difficulties.

10. **Keep a register of parents' skills; ask them how they think they can support the pre-school**

    The parents of a child with special/additional may need to be in the pre-school more or for longer periods than other parents. It is worthwhile finding out if they have any skills that they can offer the setting. This is often useful when the child is settling into the pre-school as a parent busy elsewhere but still in the room gives the key worker a chance to build her own relationship with the child. Often parents have many skills and areas of expertise that they would love to share.

11. **Ask parents to contribute to record-keeping**

    All parents know their child better than anyone. The parents of a child with special/additional needs have a better overview of their child than anyone else. They are aware of even the smallest progress. It is worthwhile sharing any record-keeping and the findings of observations with parents. Ask them if they have noted the same progress or difficulties at home. Discuss ways to move their child forward with them.

12. **Establish a pattern of talking to parents about everyday matters. This will make it easier to discuss difficult issues**

    When sensitive matters need to be discussed with parents a well established partnership between practitioner and parents is invaluable. Parents will be more inclined to trust a practitioner and acknowledge any difficulties highlighted before working together to resolve any difficulties. Remember when having what may be a difficult meeting, make sure you and the parent have the time as well as a private place to talk.

13. **Deal with issues and difficulties the same day as they occur**

    Discussing incidents or difficulties several days after they have occurred do little to improve parental relations. Daily feedback always starting with a positive should be the regular routine for parental relations.

14. **Remind parents about agreements, payments, etc. in a way that is non-embarrassing**
Practitioners who have sound relationships with parents will find it easier to have other conversations about sensitive issues. These conversations may be in regard to payments, lateness, etc. The key is sensitivity and privacy.

15. **Support parents to get to know each other by introductions, coffee mornings, socials, etc.**
Often (not always) the parents of children with special/additional needs have had less chance to make friends in the local community than other parents. This may be due to prolonged hospital stays, visits, etc. The pre-school can provide an invaluable role in helping parents and their children make new relationships and friendships.

16. **Tell parents who their child is friendly with and encourage play dates**
By raising the positive profile of a child with special/additional needs within the pre-school setting practitioners play a positive part in ensuring the child makes relationships with his/her peers. These relationships can be further extended by telling parents who their child is friendly with. Once both sets of parents are aware of childhood friendships often they will encourage the relationship by inviting each other to play dates, parties, etc. When practitioners display a positive attitude to a child with special/additional needs and their family, this often gives the parents of other children in the setting the confidence to try to get to know them better.

17. **Encourage parents to tell you social stories about their child**
Background information about children and their lives is invaluable for any practitioner. By sharing social or home stories, practitioners are looking beyond the special or additional need and begin to see the whole child. By asking about and listening to such stories a practitioner will go a long way in improving relationships with parents.

18. **Set up a small comfortable 'Parents' Space' for parents waiting or settling their children**
Often (not always) the parents of children with special/additional needs will spend longer periods of time in the pre-school, settling their children, perhaps staying if their child is unsettled or under the weather. It is beneficial to set aside a 'Parents' Space' within your pre-school. This space could also be used as a quieter place to talk to parents. The ideal Parents' Space would include a comfortable chair, some toys (for younger siblings), some magazines including educational magazines, a photograph album of outings, a parents' notice board, etc.

19. **Hold an annual parent/child event such as a concert or a picnic**
When organising such an event practitioners should be mindful of the needs of any children with special/additional needs. If in doubt discuss ideas with parents. The families of children with special/additional needs often have busy diaries which can be full of a succession of hospital appointments, sessions with speech and language therapists, physiotherapists, etc. Make sure parents have plenty of notice of the date of any trip.

20. **Have a notice board for parents' use only**
A parents' notice board allows parents the opportunity to communicate with each other. They may choose to put such things as 'looking for a nanny share' or 'selling a child's bed' etc. on the board. The parents of a child with special/additional needs should feel free, and be encouraged, to put information about any organisations' events they may be involved in such as the National Deaf Children's Society or the National Autistic Society etc.

**Further reading**

Department for Education and Employment (2001) *The Special Educational Needs Code of Practice*. DfEE.

Department for Education and Skills (2003) *Every Child Matters*. DfES.

Department for Education and Skills (2004) *Removing Barriers to Achievement: The Government Strategy for SEN*. DfES.

Department for Education and Skills (2007) *Early Years Foundation Stage: Setting the Standards for Learning, Development and Care for Children from Birth to Five*. DfES.

# CHAPTER TWO

# The toolkit: developing your own personal skills

The aim of this chapter is to support *individual* practitioners to develop the necessary skills required both to meet the needs of children with special/additional needs and to lay solid foundations for working in close partnership with parents.

The chapter sets out guidance on:

▶ Developing empathy with parents

▶ How to achieve a respectful and non-judgemental approach when working with parents

▶ Developing good listening skills

▶ How to ask effective questions and begin to reframe language

▶ Using positive body language

▶ How to reflect and grow as a professional through auditing your skills and knowledge and making a personal plan

It also offer a hands-on activity.

## Building your own personal toolkit

In order to be a successful practitioner it is necessary to have a variety of skills which enable you to be effective in your work.

This section aims to support practitioners to develop their own 'personal toolkit'. Practitioners will add their own skills as they gain experience and develop reflective practice.

You will find below a starter kit which will help build strong foundations when working with the parents of children with special/additional needs.

The following pages will explain what is meant by each aspect of the toolkit and will support you to develop your own.

1 **Empathy**

2 **Respect for families and a non-judgemental attitude**

3 **Good listening skills**

4 **Effective questions and reframing**

5 **Positive body language**

6 **Reflecting and growing**

# Empathy

Empathy involves showing compassion and understanding towards the parents of a child with special/additional needs.

When developing empathy a practitioner must attempt to understand the feelings and experience of the child and the child's parents. The way a parent may be feeling will depend on what is happening in their life in relation to their child at any given moment in time. The simplest way to do this is to imagine yourself in their place and consider their feelings and concerns in any given situation.

Empathy is not feeling sorry for a person and treating them with sympathy. Instead, it is a positive emotion that helps give you insight.

> *Empathy involves the inner experience of sharing in and comprehending the psychological state of another person.* (Hoffman, 1987: 48)

## Developing an understanding of how parents may be feeling

The diagram on the next page outlines some of the ways parents may be feeling. The place on the diagram that best describes parents' feelings and responses will vary at different times and parents may experience several of the emotions described simultaneously.

*Note*: Some parents may not experience their situation as outlined in the diagram as, like their children, all parents are different and experience things in their own unique way.

The purpose of the diagram is to outline the variety and range of emotions parents *may* experience in order for practitioners to develop their empathetic skills.

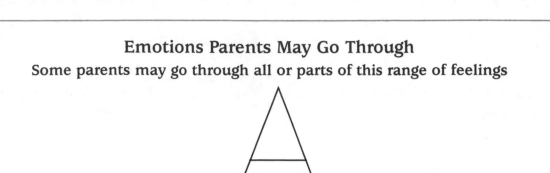

# Emotions Parents May Go Through
## Some parents may go through all or parts of this range of feelings

Securing the
best for their child

Positive and practical

Becoming well informed

Adjustment to the new reality

Fear and anxiety

Guilt

Sadness and/or anger

Denial

Shock

The diagram outlines some of the ways parents *may* be feeling at any given moment. Where parents are on the diagram (if they are there at all) will vary at different times depending upon circumstances, for example:

▶ When settling their child into a setting a parent may return to feeling *fear and anxiety* about how their child will fit into the pre-school.

▶ Parents may feel *sadness and/or anger* at the attitude of some staff or other parents with regard to their child.

▶ Particular events such as requesting a statutory assessment may prompt parents into behaving in a *positive and practical way*.

## Shock

When some parents hear or realise that their child has a special/additional need, the feelings they may have at that moment is one of complete shock. Such news may come like a bolt from the blue and parents can be stunned and upset. For some parents this news is given after birth and for others much later when a child is diagnosed by a paediatrician or other specialist.

## Denial

Parents may initially reject any professional opinion and refuse to accept it. Advice may be sought from many different sources by parents who are looking for an explanation as to why professionals seem to be 'labelling' their child. Some time may pass before parents accept that there may be difficulties ahead.

## Sadness and/or anger

Parents may feel immense grief and sadness when they realise that their child may have a special/additional need. They may feel enraged that this could be their own reality for the foreseeable future and that things have not gone as they had planned. These feelings can be exasperated by the struggle many parents have to achieve the best possible care and education for their child.

## Guilt

Often parents feel that they are to blame for any difficulties their child may experience, although this is seldom the case in reality. They may reproach themselves for not noticing things sooner or feel guilty about having to leave their child in hospital or even at the pre-school.

## Fear and anxiety

It is often with trepidation that many parents approach any new situation. How will they care for their child? Will the pre-school be able to meet their child's needs? What will the future hold for their child?

Anxiety may make parents apprehensive about leaving their child. It may make parents feel nervous and look for reassurance that practitioners understand and can cope with the needs of their child.

### Adjustment to the new reality

Parents, who, as all practitioners realise, know their child better than anyone, may have had concerns and worries about their child over a long period of time. Having a clearer understanding of their child's needs outlined by a doctor or other professional often comes as a relief to many parents. Once they know what they are dealing with they can start to readjust to their situation. This readjustment often will affect the whole family including grandparents, aunts and uncles as well as siblings.

### Become well informed

Parents of a child with a special or additional need frequently become extremely well informed about their child's condition. They themselves can become experts. Parents often make the huge efforts needed to become well informed to help them meet the challenges of and give the best possible care and attention to their child.

### Securing the best for their child

All parents – and particularly the parents of children with a special/additional need – want the best possible start for their child. In attempting to secure this, parents may often be perceived by practitioners as demanding. Through working closely together in partnership practitioners will begin to realise that parental input is vital to ensure a child with special/additional needs reaches their own potential.

Parents know the child best. They understand their child and the challenge for many parents once their child goes to pre-school is to bring practitioners 'on board'. Practitioners who are prepared to consult with and learn from parents' help provide the best possible start for any child with special/additional needs.

## Respect for families and a non-judgemental attitude

At the heart of any positive working relationship lies a genuine respect for the families of the children in your setting. It recognises that the family, and parents in particular, are the most important element in a child's life.

Sometimes this is hard to do when parents are perceived as being demanding of a practitioner's time and energy. However, basic human respect and professionalism are at the very core of care and education. All early years practitioners are in the profession because of a desire to help achieve the best possible start for the children in their care.

Being non-judgemental involves thinking positively about parents, regardless of their personal characteristics, child-rearing practices or situation. It requires a practitioner to believe that parents have a fundamental desire to do the best for their child.

A non-judgemental and respectful practitioner communicates confidence that the parents are managing often-difficult situations well. The main beneficiary of this positive relationship is always the child.

 **Case study**

Pam is Sarah's key worker. Sarah is 4 years old and has a hearing loss. She wears hearing aids in both ears. Pam wears an amplifier in the pre-school to help Sarah to pick up her voice more effectively.

Pam is a conscientious practitioner and has, over time, built up a good working relationship with Sarah's parents.

Pam noted that at her local college of further education they were running a course in British Sign Language. Pam decided she would enrol to begin to learn how to sign.

When Pam told Sarah's mother of her intentions she said: 'Good for you, but once you learn how to sign, please don't use it with Sarah as we want her to communicate through lip reading and spoken language only'.

Pam was shocked at Sarah's mother's response but kept her views to herself. She was not judgemental but accepted the decision Sarah's family had made. Pam remained Sarah's key worker and maintained a positive relationship with Sarah's parents.

Pam did, however, go ahead and learned how to sign. Later in her career she used it successfully with another child.

# Good listening skills

## Make time to listen

Do not always feel obliged to make yourself 100 per cent available to meet parents. Occasionally it is best to rearrange a discussion for when you can find a quiet place to talk. Talking in an environment which is calm and comfortable always leads to more positive outcomes. Sometimes a practitioner will need time to think how she is going to respond or sometimes will need the time to take advice from others.

*Acknowledge the parents' feeling* at the moment of contact by saying 'Yes I can see we need to talk about your concerns but I would like to talk to you when the pre-school is quieter and I can give you my full attention.'

## Reflecting back what a parent has said

In order to ensure there are no misunderstandings between practitioners and parents, throughout conversations with a parent, it is useful to get into the habit of summarising the points parents may make.

Do this by saying 'Am I right in thinking you are saying …' or 'Sorry but can I just clarify that you mean …' or any other similar phrase.

Using this strategy of reflective listening will ensure both parent and practitioner have a clear and shared understanding of what has been said.

## Resist recounting your own experiences

You may have been in a similar situation as the parent you are talking to or you may know of another family with similar difficulties. Despite this it is often not useful to 'tell your own story'.

Parents want to talk to you about *their* child and *their* difficulties.

## Acknowledging a parent's feelings or emotions

Recognising and acknowledging how parents are feeling can immediately give comfort and reassurance and often deflects a difficult situation.

Use phrases like 'I can see you're upset' or 'I know you would like the situation to be better' or 'Yes I can see that you are angry about what has happened'.

Acknowledging a feeling does not mean you agree, but it does mean you are open to discussion and are aware of how a parent may be feeling.

## Active listening

Good listening involves listening to what is being said as well as *how* it is being said.

Good active listening helps avoid any misunderstanding of the message. Some elements of active listening involve reflecting back (see above), pauses and sometimes silence, nodding, good but not oppressive eye contact, controlled body language and the effective use of questions (see asking open ended-questions outlined overleaf).

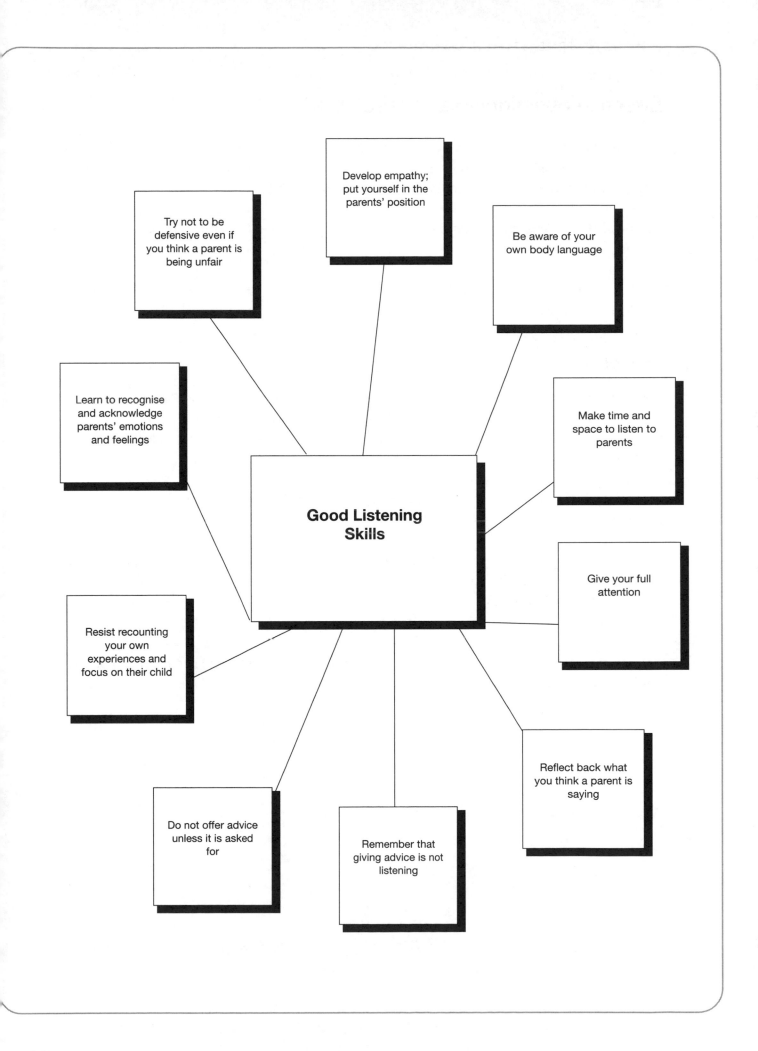

Try not to be defensive even if you think a parent is being unfair

Develop empathy; put yourself in the parents' position

Be aware of your own body language

Learn to recognise and acknowledge parents' emotions and feelings

Make time and space to listen to parents

**Good Listening Skills**

Give your full attention

Resist recounting your own experiences and focus on their child

Reflect back what you think a parent is saying

Do not offer advice unless it is asked for

Remember that giving advice is not listening

# Effective questioning and reframing

Effective questioning will help practitioners to stay in the picture about a particular child. It can be also provide insight into how a parent may be feeling, clarify what has been said or done, and allow practitioners to plan in the best interests of the child.

*Open-ended questions* encourage people to talk, invite further information and allow parents to express what are their most relevant and important concerns.

On the next page is a list of *open questions* that, if used in the right context, will support parents to talk about their child in their own way.

## Reframing

Reframing can sometimes be used by an experienced practitioner to help parents view something in a new and more positive way. This can mean that during an exchange with parents the practitioner can choose to focus on the positive aspects of a situation and give less attention to a negative, or to highlight a small step of progress.

For example, if a parent describes their child as 'stubborn', the practitioner may say 'Yes he is persistent and this often helps him to complete activities successfully rather than give up'.

Another example is when a parent shows disappointment because their child has not yet started eating snack at pre-school. The practitioner can point out progress by saying 'Yes but he has started to look at or touch the food of his peers, I think this is a positive step in the right direction'.

*Note*: When using this strategy be careful that you don't talk over or negate parents' concerns. Remember to 'acknowledge the feeling'.

# Open Questions to Use with Parents

❭ Tell me about ................. (child's name)

❭ What can we do to help ................. to settle in?

❭ What types of activities does ............... like to do?

❭ What sorts of things are challenging for ............. ?

❭ What concerns you most about ................ coming here every day?

❭ What types of changes have you noticed since ................. started here?

❭ What can we do to keep you informed about how ................... is doing?

❭ How do you manage toileting at home? Do you think we should do that here?

❭ What makes ................. happy and content?

❭ Are you confident we are doing enough to meet ................. needs?

❭ Is there anything else that you would like us to know about ............... ?

 *Working with Parents of Children with Special Educational Needs,. Paul Chapman Publishing © Chris Dukes and Maggie Smith, 2007*

## Positive body language

For all of us body language occurs subconsciously but those subconscious movements often send powerful messages to the person we are talking to.

For instance, have you ever been purchasing an item in a shop and the assistant is obviously listening to a conversation her colleagues may be having while serving you? She is so engrossed that she barely makes eye contact with you? You quite rightly feel offended as, after all, you are a paying customer and you will probably also feel the need to look at your receipt and change to check she has not made a mistake.

The tips below on the dos and don'ts of body language will help practitioners avoid obvious pitfalls when talking to parents. The main point, however, is to be alert and give your full attention to the person you are talking with.

# The Dos and Don'ts of Body language

## Do

▶ Give your full attention.

▶ Be aware of yourself and the image you are projecting.

▶ Smile and try to be friendly (if appropriate).

▶ Nod your head (not vigorously) when a parent is talking to you – this gives a signal that you are listening.

▶ Have consistent (but not intrusive) eye contact.

▶ Have a relaxed open posture.

▶ Stand straight.

▶ Hold your arms loosely with your palms up and out (this is a totally non-aggressive and non-challenging stance).

## Don't

▶ Show shock or disapproval at anything a parent may say.

▶ Be distracted by other things that are happening in the room.

▶ Look at your watch. (If you do, explain why.)

▶ Hold your fists tight or clenched.

▶ Fold your arms.

▶ Stand too close to a parent – be aware of personal space.

▶ Sigh or look bored.

**Hands-on activity**

During staff meetings take five minutes out to role play and practise good listening skills and body language.

In pairs act out the following scenarios:

1. Mrs Sori has stopped to talk to you at home time. You are standing at the setting door calling children out of the room to meet up with their parents. She says: 'I have had a hospital appointment today and have had some bad news'.

2. Mr Blunt appears during your story time. You are on the carpet with six children who are all enjoying the story. He says: 'What did Joe have to eat this morning? I told you he was not allowed any milk products' (he seems a bit agitated).

3. During a progress meeting Mrs Alone starts to cry and says she is finding it difficult to cope at home. You are surprised and shocked at her behaviour as she has always struck you as a very capable and well-organised person.

## Reflecting and growing

The ability to have an open mind and a desire to move on in your own practice is a solid foundation for building positive relationships with parents. Sometimes parents will be able to support a practitioner to fill knowledge gaps about their child's special/additional needs. This can be by giving them information about a condition or showing them how to undertake activities or care skills. It could be demonstrating a physiotherapy programme or how to support a child's feeding or toileting.

Parents can help practitioners in other ways such as by signposting the way to further information or support organisations, by introducing them to other professionals, sharing reports and assessments.

Sometimes, however, for a variety of reasons, parents are not able to share skills or be supportive of a practitioner. In these cases practitioners need to find out for themselves as much information about specific conditions and any additional needs that a child may have.

It is generally regarded as good practice to gain as much insight as possible into a child's needs prior to admission. This helps practitioners plan for a child's arrival. It also supports practitioners in carrying out a fair assessment of the level of support a child may need for a successful placement. Any candid assessment that is being carried out in the setting should include a skills evaluation of the proposed key worker, SENCO and even the manager. This will allow for personal action plans to be written for individuals involved with the child.

Such an assessment or audit of skills should always be viewed in a positive way by practitioners. It will provide the perfect opportunity to honestly reflect upon your own skills and knowledge and lead to your own professional development.

No one can be an expert in every area of special educational needs but everyone can undertake simple research, look for practical advice and attend training.

The 'Audit and Action Plan' on the following pages is intended to help practitioners reflect upon gaps in their knowledge regarding a child's needs as well as to help highlight the skills required by individual practitioners to meet these needs (*Audit columns 1 and 2*).

# Questions to Consider for My Audit and Action Plan

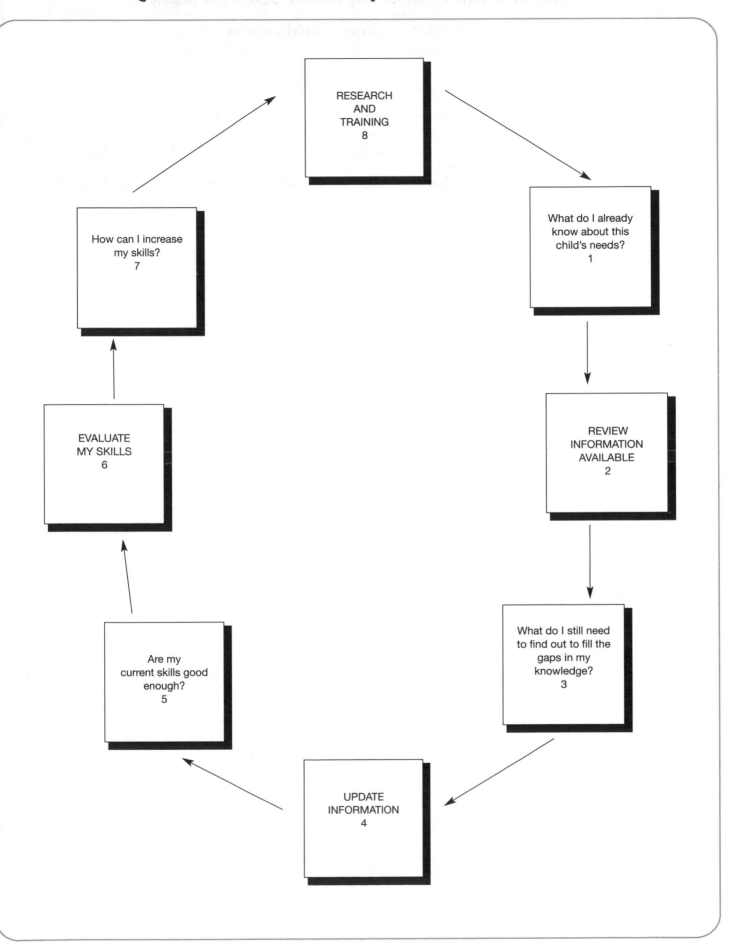

RESEARCH
AND
TRAINING
8

What do I already
know about this
child's needs?
1

How can I increase
my skills?
7

REVIEW
INFORMATION
AVAILABLE
2

EVALUATE
MY SKILLS
6

What do I still need
to find out to fill the
gaps in my
knowledge?
3

Are my
current skills good
enough?
5

UPDATE
INFORMATION
4

## Audit and Action Plan for Key Worker, SENCO or Manager

### *Information* about a child's needs

Child's name ...................................................................................

| Audit | Audit | My Action Plan |
|---|---|---|
| What do I already know? | What do I need to find out? | How and when will I get this information? |
|  |  |  |

## Audit and Action Plan for Key Worker, SENCO or Manager

### *Skills* needed to meet a child's needs

Practitioner's name ...................................................................................

| Audit | Audit | My Action Plan |
|---|---|---|
| What skills do I currently have that will support this child? | What extra skills will I need? | How and when can I get these new skills? |
| | | |

An Action Plan (*column 3*) can then be written to help plan for the acquisition of increased information and practical skills.

The chart will help you see that by asking yourself the right questions, a plan can be easily completed and carried out.

## How to use the Audit and Action Plans

Tanya is 3 years old and is due to start in the pre-school which her mother wants her to attend every morning. Tanya has a form of cerebral palsy. Her mother has described the main points of her condition as:

▶ favouring one side of the body over the other;

▶ poor muscle control and lack of coordination;

▶ muscle spasms or seizures;

▶ oral problems such as sucking, chewing and swallowing.

Tanya loves to play with play dough, dress up and join in singing and story time.

Susan is going to become Tanya's key worker.

As part of the admissions procedure the setting SENCO/manager has asked Susan (key worker) to fill in the audits (see the sample completed Audit and Action Plans on the following pages). These will be used to help support and prepare Susan for becoming Tanya's key worker.

## Audit and Action Plan for Key Worker, SENCO or Manager

### *Information* about a child's needs

Child's name ..........Tanya..................................................

| Audit | Audit | My Action Plan |
|---|---|---|
| What do I already know? | What do I need to find out? | How and when will I get this information? |
| ▶ Tanya has cerebral palsy | ▶ More about Tanya's condition, e.g what type of cerebral palsy, and how it will affect her nursery life | ▶ At the professionals' meeting, through reading all of the reports given to me and following visits to the setting by Tanya and her mum. I may need to go on specific training |
| ▶ Tanya has a physiotherapy programme in place | ▶ How often and who carries out this programme | ▶ Ask Tanya's mum during the home visit. Can I observe a session? |
| ▶ Tanya is not yet toilet trained | ▶ Is this related to her condition? | ▶ Through my own research, talking to Tanya's mum and the other professionals involved |
| ▶ Tanya has previously attended a playgroup 2 mornings a week | ▶ What measures did that setting put in place for Tanya? | ▶ Obtain parental permission and ring the previous setting and/or invite them to a transition 'in' meeting at our setting |

Practitioner's name ........................ *Susan* ......................................................

| Audit | Audit | My Action Plan |
|---|---|---|
| What skills do I currently have will support this child? | What extra skills will I need? | How and when can I get these new skills? |
| ▶ I have key worked a child with SEN previously and know how to write an IEP | ▶ How to liaise with outside professionals and include their advice in my work with Tanya | ▶ Make sure I attend all professionals' meetings here in the setting and carry out visits. Participate in any training made available. Talk to our area SENCO and our setting SENCO and ask for guidance |
| ▶ I am good at research and have good computer skills | ▶ Specific websites to look at, and books that will offer me guidance | ▶ I will start with the cerebral palsy charity www.scope.org.uk |
| | | ▶ I will ask the other professionals involved for any leaflets or books they can recommend |
| | | ▶ I will ask my manager for an allowance to buy guidance materials and some free time for research |
| ▶ I am good at differentiating the curriculum | ▶ I need to find out what type of activities and equipment will best support Tanya's development | ▶ I will audit our materials and books making sure they are suitable for Tanya. I will spend one-on-one time with Tanya and her mother to find out what she likes doing and use that as my starting point |

**Further reading**

Bolton, R. (1986) *People Skills: How to Assert Yourself, Listen to Others and Resolve Conflicts*. Simon & Schuster.

Pease, A. and Pease, B. (2006) *The Definitive Book of Body Language: The Hidden Meaning Behind People's Gestures and Expressions*. Bantam.

# CHAPTER THREE
# Building blocks: planning, policies and practice

The aim of this chapter is to support each pre-school setting to put in place the necessary building blocks for working in partnership with parents. This will not only enable you to welcome and include children with special/additional needs but also to build successful relationships with their parents.

In this chapter you will find the sample policies and guidance which form those building blocks together with advice on how to put them into practice.

The chapter sets out guidance on:

▶ First impressions – how to recognise an inclusive setting

▶ Your inclusion policy

▶ Admissions and settling in

▶ Gathering information

▶ Home visits

▶ Preparing for a child's arrival

▶ Transitions – moving on

▶ Issues of confidentiality

It also offers suggestions for hands-on activities.

# First impressions

When parents are visiting pre-schools and looking for the right place to send their child, *first impressions do count*. This is especially important for parents of children with special/additional needs who may have extra anxieties about whether their child will be welcome at a setting or if their particular needs can be met.

Initially parents may just have a quick chat and a tour of the nursery, so it is important that the inclusive attitudes and ethos of your pre-school are evident to everyone who visits, for however short a time.

'Twenty Ways to Recognise an Inclusive Setting' is a good starting point for you to think about what parents of children with special or additional needs might look for and what sort of first impression your pre-school and staff might make.

# 20 Ways to Recognise an Inclusive Setting

1.  The setting is used by a wide cross-section of the local community.

2.  The staff are flexible and responsive and team work is evident.

3.  The environment has been carefully considered in terms of accessibility.

4.  Practitioners have time to reflect and discuss their practice.

5.  Strong links exist between the setting and community.

6.  Good use is made of LA and heath service professionals.

7.  Staff attend outside training and have regular in-house training sessions.

8.  A key worker system is being used.

9.  The setting Special Educational Needs Coordinator (SENCO) has the time and resources to carry out their duties effectively.

10. Pictures and displays represent a diverse society.

11. Staff have criteria for choosing equipment and books.

12. Transition in and out of the setting is well established and effective.

13. Planning is led by the interests and needs of the children who attend the setting.

14. Children's views are sought both informally and formally, especially regarding individual targets.

15. Each parent/carer feels valued by practitioners; their views and opinions are regularly sought.

16. The setting has a vision and ethos which includes meeting the needs of those children with additional needs.

17. The setting is well oganised with good policies and procedures in place.

18. All children are equally welcome to attend.

19. Staff have developed sound methods of communicating with parents.

20. Procedures are in place to support staff to identify children who may have an additional need.

# An inclusion policy

Every pre-school setting that receives nursery funding is required to have a Special Educational Needs policy or Inclusion policy (see the 'Sample Inclusion Policy' on the next page). This policy should support the inclusive attitude and environment that you create. It outlines the procedures and practices that are in place to support children with special/additional needs in your setting. It should mention working in partnership with parents and should be available alongside your other policies for all parents to see.

 **Hands-on activities**

1. Consider what first impression your pre-school might give to a prospective parent or a visiting professional. Look at your general environment, accessibility, books and displays and most importantly staff attitudes.

   Think about any improvements you might need to make.

2. Look at your pre-school's Inclusion policy.

   ▶ Does it mention working in partnership with parents?

   ▶ Does it reflect the practice in your setting?

   ▶ Is it reviewed regularly?

# Sample Inclusion Policy

Here at ............ we want all of our children to have the best possible learning opportunities and experiences. We welcome and actively promote inclusive practices and diversity within our setting. Our aim is to make our setting accessible to all families who wish to use it.

We have due regard to the Special Educational Needs Code of Practice 2001 and comply with the requirements of the Disability Discrimination Act 1995.

Within our pre-school we endeavour to provide an inclusive environment and curriculum that enables all children to fully participate in the activities and experiences on offer.

We work in partnership with parents and other agencies, where appropriate, to support individual children's learning. We aim to provide effective support to meet every child's needs.

Our manager and Special Educational Needs Coordinator (SENCO) are responsible for the implementation and annual review of our Inclusion policy. They ensure that all staff, students and parents are aware of the policy and we welcome discussion about individual children or any other matters arising from the policy.

Our present SENCO is ..................................................................

and he/she is responsible for the day-to-day organisation of any matters regarding children with special/additional needs.

It is, however, the responsibility of all staff to plan for, work with and support all children whatever their needs.

Early identification

▶ Through our record-keeping and comprehensive system of regular observations we are able to recognise any additional needs a child may have. We always in the first instance discuss any concerns with parents and together plan an appropriate plan of action and support. This will be regularly monitored by our SENCO.

▶ Children who have an identified additional need on joining the setting will be welcomed and celebrated in the same way as all of our children. An individual settling-in plan will be devised by staff and parents. Suitable levels of support will be offered and input and advice from other agencies and professionals will be sought. The SENCO will take responsibility for co-ordinating this – working closely alongside parents.

# Moving in or moving on

## Supporting parents through transitions

Times of transition such as moving from home into an early years setting, changing pre-school or transferring from such a setting into school can be anxious times for both child and parent.

Above all parents should be encouraged to consider carefully all the choices and options available so that they can make the best decision for their child. Often this will include practicalities such as getting to and from the setting or school, other children in the family, childcare, working hours, as well as what a setting has to offer their child.

While *all* parents of *all* children have anxieties about changes in their child's lives, for parents of children with special educational needs these can often be magnified.

Additional concerns usually centre on:

▶ if their child will be made welcome;

▶ if staff teams have any knowledge of their child's particular condition or needs;

▶ if staff are aware of how their child's needs might affect their learning or behaviour;

▶ if their child will be 'understood' by a new set of staff;

▶ if adequate support will be in place;

▶ if any one person will be taking particular responsibility for their child;

▶ who they can talk to if they are worried or concerned.

Nearly all these fears can be avoided or parents reassured by careful planning and preparation. This is the key to good transition, whatever a child's age, stage or difficulties. The best settings are those who have a welcoming, well organised and flexible approach to children who have special or additional needs so that parents feel able to discuss their child's needs before they start and can continue a positive dialogue which has the child at the centre.

A 'can do' attitude is important; however, there are also practical steps which can be taken to ensure that a child starting at your setting, or moving on to another setting or to school, has the best possible chance of a successful transition. Most of these can easily be built into the everyday practice at your setting and it is helpful to have a written admissions and settling-in procedure which both staff and parents are aware of.

# Moving in: admissions and settling in

Parents of children with special/additional needs are often anxious about making the right choices for their child. They need to be reassured that your setting is the right place for their child.

The fact that some children take longer than others to settle into the pre-school should be discussed during pre-admission meetings. Parents should be reassured that they will be supported for as long as it takes to settle their child.

Children cannot play or learn successfully if they are anxious and unhappy. Settling-in procedures should aim to help parents to help their children to feel comfortable in the pre-school.

Children with a special/additional need may have additional experiences that mean that settling in might need extra planning and thought.

For example, a child with special/additional needs may have:

▶ undergone several admissions to hospital;

▶ attended many appointments with several professionals;

▶ had less opportunity to socialise with his/her peers;

▶ have specialist requirements;

▶ have developmental delay and resulting immaturity.

Admissions and settling-in procedures for individual children therefore need to be very well planned.

## Ways to gather information

▶ Have a well designed *admissions pro-forma* that asks the right sort of questions.
(See the sample supplementary admissions pro-forma 'More about Me' on the following pages to add to your own admissions form.

▶ Carry out a *home visit*, if the child's parents agree.
Try to make home visits an essential part of your admissions procedures, especially when a new child has a special or additional need. Build time into the start of or end of term to carry out home visits.

▶ With parental permission *contact all professionals* involved to ask for advice, including your area SENCO and early support key worker if the child has one. (Ask the parents to put you in contact.)

▶ Hold an *information-sharing meeting*.
A meeting with other professionals involved with the child and the pre-school staff could prove invaluable to the settling-in process.

It is always a good idea to write down beforehand any questions you need to ask during the meeting.

# More about me

My name ...........................................

My date of birth ..................................................

Other playgroups and pre-schools I have been to (names and addresses):


At home I speak (language):


I also use other things to help me communicate (please list Makaton, PECS, etc.):


The name and address of my GP is:

```



```

The name and address of my Health Visitor is:

```



```

I sometimes go to the hospital and usually see these people:

Hospital name and address:

My doctors are:

These are the names of some of the other people I see sometimes (e.g. speech and language therapists, specialist teachers, etc.):

I sometimes need help with my:

▶   Speech

▶   Toileting

▶   Vision

▶   Hearing

▶   Walking

▶   Behaviour

▶   Other (please outline)

I have:

▶ Allergies (please outline)

▶ Asthma

▶ Dietary requirements (please outline)

▶ Other needs (please outline)

I regularly take these medicines:

Some other important medical information about me includes the following (please outline):

Some other things you might like to know about me:

Things I like to do:

Things I find difficult:

Parent's signature................................................ Date.......................

# Home visits

Home visits can prove to be invaluable especially in building the foundations of a strong partnership with the parents of a child with special/additional needs.

Early years staff make home visits as it is a recognised and proven way to better meet the needs of a child and family. It promotes partnership between parents and practitioners. They allow for informal meeting and discussion in the parents' own environment. This in turn supports parental involvement once the child starts at the pre-school.

Effective home visits benefit the pre-school setting, child and parent.

The key to successful home visiting is:

▶ planning;

▶ clarity of purpose (shared with parents);

▶ ability to listen to parents.

## Uses of home visits

Home visits can be used in several ways

▶ As an introduction and 'getting to know you' session prior to the child starting at the pre-school, usually carried out by the key worker and the SENCO together. *Two members of staff should always visit together.* **This is the most common type of home visit**.

▶ As an observational tool for the practitioner to see a child in their own environment.

▶ As a learning tool. This is when the practitioner learns a new skill or technique from the parent by watching how it is done at home.

▶ As a 'safe' place for parents to hold a meeting with pre-school staff, perhaps to review the term or discuss issues arising.

▶ As an outreach service if the child is ill at home (this can also include hospital visits). Funding often allows for this if the child has a Statement of Special Educational Needs.

Some pre-schools will choose to home visit all of the children starting at their pre-school while some may choose to visit only specific families.

If a child is starting at your pre-school with identified special/additional needs it is a good idea to try to make a home visit.

*Note:* Home visits can be made only if parents agree to practitioners visiting their home – they can never be compulsory.

## Planning a home visit

The first thing to do is ask yourself the question: 'What is the purpose of my home visit?' Once your intention is clear you will be able to explain it to the parents.

Some reasons may be:

▶ to get to know the child and parent better;

▶ to agree with parents a settling-in plan for the child;

▶ to get a better overview of the child's needs;

▶ to learn from parents how to undertake specific care tasks in relation to the child;

▶ to inform parents about your setting's routines, activities, etc.;

▶ to meet the child and other family members who may visit your setting from time to time, e.g. grandparents;

▶ to meet with other professionals and parents in an information sharing/planning session.

Home visits need to be well planned.

1. **Parents need to be contacted and asked if they agree to a home visit**. At this stage state the purpose of the visit (see above), say how long the visit will last and suggest that parents may want to add their own items to the agenda for the visit. Ask them to think about a date and say you will ring them in a week's time to confirm. (This avoids putting parents on the spot.) Ring back at the appointed time and agree a date

2. **Confirm this date and the purpose of the visit in writing** (see the 'Home Visit Sample Letter of Introduction' on page 52).

3. **Preparation for the staff who are home visiting** (see also 'Top Tips for Staff Who Carry Out Home Visits' on page 51):

   – Meet with the person who is visiting with you to agree on the order of the visit. For example, sometimes the key worker will play with the child and get to know them while the SENCO will fill out forms etc. with the parent.

   – Remind yourself of the names of the child and parent.

   – Research any special/additional needs issues.

   – Plan travel arrangements.

   – Discuss dress code.

   – Does a translator need to be in place? (If so ask the parents to arrange for a relative or friend to be present to translate.)

   – Gather toys, photograph albums, leaflets, forms, etc. together.

   – Leave schedule of visit/s and emergency contact details with the manager in the pre-school.

4. **On arrival:**

   – Introduce self.

   – Establish social relations by engaging in some 'social chit chat'.

   – Try to appear comfortable.

5. **During the visit:**

   – Review the purpose of the visit to parents.

   – Ask parents if they would like to add other items to the list.

   – Share information and try to do all of the things agreed. (This may not always be possible as it is easy to get sidetracked during a home visit.)

   – Towards the end of the visit summarise all of the things discussed and ask parents if they have any questions.

   – Keep to your agreed time (even if not finished – suggest a follow-up talk at the pre-school).

6. **After the visit:**

   – Follow up on any things that you said you would do/get for parents.

   – Debrief the information received to your manager.

   – Use the information received to plan for the child's needs.

 **Hands-on activity**

Write a paragraph explaining to prospective parents why you like to carry out home visits prior to admissions for children with special/additional needs.

Add it to your setting's prospectus.

# Top Tips for Staff Who Carry Out Home Visits

## Do

▶ Visit with another member of staff.

▶ Have a specific purpose/plan for the visit.

▶ Be prepared to be flexible.

▶ Be prompt and don't overstay your welcome.

▶ Realise the limitations of your role (don't make promises you can't keep).

▶ Keep language appropriate.

▶ Dress appropriately and comfortably.

▶ Respect cultural values that may be different from your own.

▶ Be well organised and have everything with you that you need.

▶ Ask parents to remove pets if you are not comfortable with them.

▶ Try to be yourself.

## Don't

▶ Do all of the talking (encourage parents to tell you about their child).

▶ Bring other visitors without asking parents first.

▶ Spend all of your precious time socialising with parents – be focused and friendly.

▶ Try to impose your ideas.

▶ Make promises you can't keep.

 *Working with Parents of Children with Special Educational Needs, Paul Chapman Publishing © Chris Dukes and Maggie Smith, 2007*

# Home Visit
## (Sample Letter of Introduction)

Name and address of your pre-school

Date

Telephone number

Re: Home Visit by Pre-School SENCO and Key Worker

Dear ...................................................

On ...... (date) ............................... at ............ (time) ........................, we would like to visit you and ...... (child's name) ............................................. in your home.

Two members of the Pre-School staff will visit you: .......... (Key worker's name) ............. (and SENCO's name) ...........................

Both of them will be carrying photographic identity.

Our visit will last about 45 minutes. During our visit we would like to discuss

.............................. (state purpose of visit) ........................................ and any other issues that you would like to discuss.

Please contact us if this is no longer convenient. Otherwise we look forward to meeting with you and .......... (child's name).

Yours sincerely

# Preparing for a child's arrival

▶ Ensure that you have enough time to prepare for a child's arrival and plan ahead for specific needs.

▶ Give the key worker and SENCO the time and opportunity to build a relationship with the child and parents.

▶ Ensure staff receive any training necessary prior to the child starting at the setting.

▶ Have in place any specialist equipment the child may need.

▶ Audit your toys and books to ensure they (or at least some of them) are suitable for the child.

## Specialist training for pre-school staff

During any home visit and/or information-sharing meeting it is essential that it is clarified whether or not any specialist training is needed for pre-school staff. This training can take the form of Epi pen training, lifting techniques, Makaton or PECS (Picture Exchange System) training, etc.

If it is agreed that such training is necessary this should be carried out prior to the child's admission if possible.

During the information-sharing meeting it should be agreed who is going to take responsibility for arranging and paying for any training. The pre-school setting as a rule-of-thumb should not incur extra costs for such staff training.

## Consideration of room layout, routines and equipment

Following a home visit and after information sharing the pre-school staff may need to consider room layout and routines. Some changes may have to be made to meet a child's needs, such as:

▶ changes to snack times;

▶ changes to story times;

▶ room layout to ensure mobility;

▶ the provision of a quiet area;

▶ toilet adaptations;

▶ changes to lighting;

▶ provision of a carpeted area;

) provision of specialist equipment;

) new and suitable toys or books.

## The employment of an extra member of staff (if funding is available)

Some children (very few) will have a statement of educational need prior to coming to your set-ting. This means they may have funding available from a local authority to be supported by an assistant while they are at your setting. Other children may be eligible for a grant or funding from the local authority. This will vary from area to area but it is a good idea to discuss the pos-sibility of any funding during a meeting with professionals such as a Portage worker or advisory teacher or your Area SENCO.

If funding is available you may be able to employ an extra member of staff to help the child be included in your pre-school. This extra person can be used in two ways:

) to free up the child's key worker to undertake specific target work with the child;

) to support the child within the setting.

The setting manager and SENCO will usually interview and supervise any extra staff and they will also make a decision about the role of the extra member of staff.

The spending of any money will usually be overseen by someone from the local authority, sometimes the Area SENCO.

*Note*: It is the SENCO and manager's responsibility to avoid the 'Velcro effect' with a support assistant. This means the assistant should not need to shadow the child all day every day, as the other members of the team should interact as much with a child with special/additional needs as they do with the other children.

## Being flexible

) Agree a clear settling-in plan with parents but be prepared to be flexible.

) Whatever plans you make, be prepared to adapt and change them once the child has started. It is not always clear initially what will work best for a child.

Remember, some children with additional needs may not have been to a toddler – or any other type of group before. The bond between them and their parents will be strong and they may be worried about being left at pre-school. So therefore extra thought has to be put into how best the child can be prepared for starting at pre-school. Below are some suggestions:

) Regular visits to the child's home by the key worker before and during settling in.

▶ Pre-school routines that are similar to home routines, especially in the area of care such as toileting and eating.

▶ A photograph album of the pre-school activities, rooms and staff for the child to look at with parents at home during the weeks prior to starting at the pre-school.

▶ Contact with some of the other children who will also be starting or who are already at the pre-school such as friends or neighbours. The setting can help facilitate this by holding a coffee morning for all new parents/carers and children.

▶ Attending drop-in sessions and any special events that the setting may be having.

A useful parent-information leaflet 'Let's Talk About … Working Together to Settle Your Child into Pre-School' is included on the following page.

# Let's Talk About ...

## Working Together to Settle Your Child into Pre-school

▶ Make sure the pre-school staff have clear and detailed information about your child's needs, medication, personal care arrangements, wider professional team, as well as their likes and dislikes. Discuss with key worker, SENCO and manager.

▶ Agree to, or ask for, a home visit to give yourself an opportunity to meet the pre-school SENCO and key worker. This also gives staff an invaluable opportunity to see your child at home.

▶ Take your time and visit the pre-school with your child as many times as you need to feel comfortable. Arrange these visits with the SENCO.

▶ Begin to feel confident that your child will be cared for as you would wish in the setting. If this is not happening please discuss with our SENCO.

▶ Agree a 'settling-in' period. This is where you stay with your child until he/she gets used to staying at the pre-school without you. Agree this with the SENCO and the key worker.

▶ Attend the setting every day with your child, building up to leaving for short periods of time until you are comfortable with leaving your child for the session. Agree this with the pre-school staff.

Your own notes:

# Moving on: preparing for school

Parents will have all of the same anxieties when a child moves on from pre-school to school. It can be particularly difficult when parents have established good relationships with early years practitioners, as they face getting to know a new set of teachers and a different environment and routine.

If practitioners have good transition procedures and have built links with local schools and staff they can be key to building a bridge between pre-school and school for both parents and child.

The same basic factors necessary for a child's successful entry into pre-school are needed for a successful transition into school.

## Gathering information

It is particularly important to explain to parents of children with special/additional needs about your policy on the transfer of information. For a variety of reasons some parents can be reluctant for information to be passed on to other settings or schools. This matter can be more easily addressed when parents and practitioners have established a good relationship. When there is mutual trust and respect most parents will agree that their child's needs and well-being are paramount and that liaison is necessary to ensure a smooth transition.

## Being prepared

Schools are just as concerned about being prepared to meet a child's needs as pre-schools. Sometimes it is the pre-school which needs to take the initiative and contact a school to perhaps invite them to visit the setting and to see a child at work and play. Where a child has an IEP/IP it can be extremely useful for the school SENCO or reception teacher to be invited to hear about a child's progress and the strategies which are successfully used to help them.

For parents, this is an extremely helpful way for practitioners to support and introduce them to school staff so that they can begin the process of building up the new relationships.

For school staff, meetings and liaison of this kind provide an opportunity to think about the kind of preparations they might need to make for the child's arrival, in terms of resources equipment, training or staffing.

## Being flexible

Early years practitioners can again help the transition process for children and reassure parents by suggesting flexible ways to help a child. This may be to do with extra visits to a new classroom or to meet the teacher or the rate and frequency of a child's entry into school during the first few weeks. Adaptations or strategies which have proved useful at the pre-school can be passed on to school staff so that they already have a good idea about how best to help a child and how to work effectively with their parents.

# Ideas for improving transitions

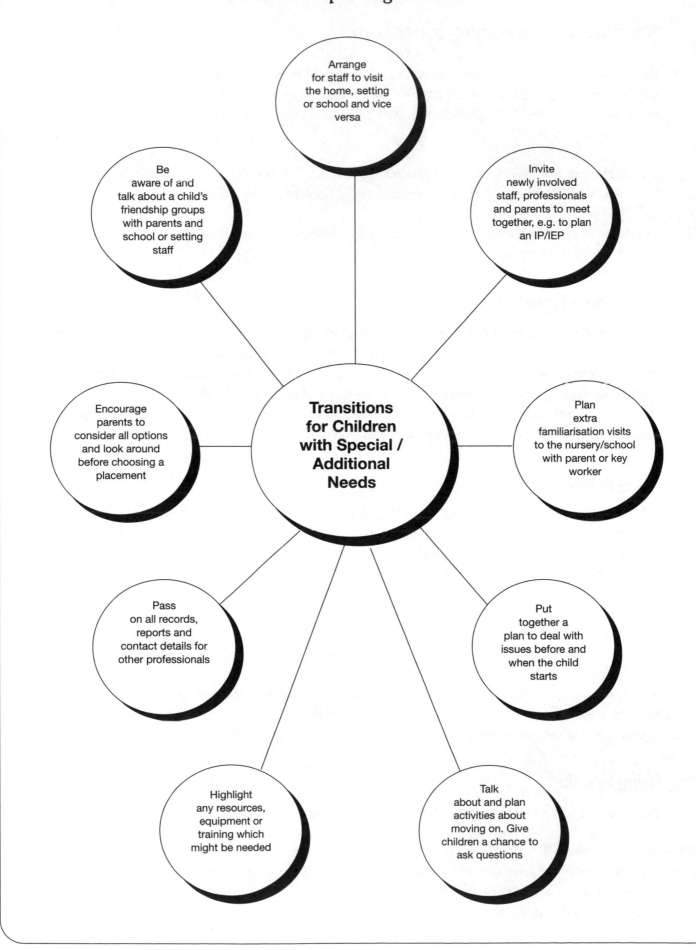

Arrange for staff to visit the home, setting or school and vice versa

Be aware of and talk about a child's friendship groups with parents and school or setting staff

Invite newly involved staff, professionals and parents to meet together, e.g. to plan an IP/IEP

Encourage parents to consider all options and look around before choosing a placement

**Transitions for Children with Special / Additional Needs**

Plan extra familiarisation visits to the nursery/school with parent or key worker

Pass on all records, reports and contact details for other professionals

Put together a plan to deal with issues before and when the child starts

Highlight any resources, equipment or training which might be needed

Talk about and plan activities about moving on. Give children a chance to ask questions

# Confidentiality issues

The key worker or SENCO, or both, will over time build up a relatively close relationship with many parents of children with special or additional needs. The relationship will often be one built on mutual respect and an appreciation of each other's circumstances and hard work.

Knowing your boundaries (page 66) helps practitioners to recognise and avoid many of the possible pitfalls of developing a professional relationship into a close friendship. However, it is our view that it is for individuals to determine the sort of relationship they want to have with parents.

Nevertheless, issues of confidentiality may arise once a practitioner becomes party to sensitive and often personal information regarding a child, their parents and the family as a whole. It is the responsibility of the setting manager, supported by the SENCO, to devise a system of information-sharing within their setting. Together they should agree on who has access to confidential information within the setting.

As a general rule-of-thumb information should be shared on a *need-to-know basis*. A child's special or additional needs should never be discussed with other parents, students (except on a need-to-know basis) or the family or friends of practitioners employed in the setting. This should be made explicit by the setting manager at interview and through internal procedures and policies.

*The exception to this rule is if there is a child protection issue. In such a case the setting's child protection procedures should be implemented immediately.*

A child's file should be kept in a locked cabinet and the Individual Education Plan should be available for planning etc. but should *never* be displayed upon the pre-school wall.

## Hands-on activity

Once you have established a good working relationship with the parents of a child with special or additional needs they may begin to share sensitive information with you.

▶ What sort of information might parents share with you?

▶ Who would you share this information with?

▶ What issues may arise?

(This activity is particularly suitable for the setting manager, SENCO and key worker to carry out together.)

**Further reading**

Department for Education and Skills (2006) *Implementing the Disability Discrimination Act in Schools and Early Years Settings*. DfES.

Dukes, C. and Smith, M. (2006) *A Practical Guide to Pre-School Inclusion*, Hands on Guide. Paul Chapman.

Books to use with children or lend to parents prior to transition into pre-school or when leaving pre-school:

Ashley, Bernard (1993) *Cleversticks*. Collins.

Fitzpatrick, Marie-Louise (2007) *Silly School*. Frances Lincoln.

Forward, Toby (2005) *The First Day of School*. Picture Corgi.

Mitchell, Rita Phillips and Ayliffe, Alex (1999) *The Gotcha Smile*. Orchard Books.

# CHAPTER FOUR
# Working together: involving parents in their children's learning

The aim of this chapter is to consider those factors that influence your working relationship with parents. It gives advice on reaching out to parents of children with additional/special educational needs and practical tips for learning from parents.

It contains a case study illustrating parents and practitioners sharing skills and working jointly to plan Individual Education Plan targets.

This chapter sets out:

▶ What parents may bring to your setting

▶ Maintaining professionalism and knowing your boundaries

▶ Reaching out to parents

▶ Individual Education Plans – involving parents

▶ Sharing skills

▶ Let's talk about IEPs – a leaflet for parents

## Working with parents of children with special/additional needs: factors to consider

Perhaps the most important thing to remember when working with parents of children with special/additional needs is that they are all individuals and need to be treated as such.

Every parent will bring a unique set of values, beliefs, attitudes, background and circumstances to your relationship, just as you do.

It is this unique set of factors which shapes how and what kind of relationship is formed between parent and practitioner. The more you get to know a parent the more you are able to understand the things they may say or do and *vice versa*. Many misunderstandings can be avoided by taking a little time to think about and appreciate a parent's perspective. You can do this, however, only if you have invested time in getting to know them and their family.

Family makeup and organisation can play an important part in determining how a parent is able to work with you. Some parents have large extended families that can provide various kinds of support. This may range from more practical help with childcare to the emotional support of a listening ear. Large families also have their demands, however, often with wider responsibilities for other siblings or dependent relatives. There may be conflicting views and advice about what might be needed to support the child with special/additional needs.

On the other hand, other parents could be raising children alone, or have a limited support system of friends or family. This can give them less choice and flexibility when settling their children, arranging meetings or volunteering to help, etc.

Work and childcare are other issues which need to be taken into account when working with parents of children with special/additional needs. There are considerable financial implications to caring for a child, particularly one with more complex special needs. Time off to attend appointments and meetings can be very difficult to arrange and there is almost always a pressure of time to either get back to work or pick up other children.

Each parent will also bring their life experience with them to any relationship they may have with you as a practitioner. Some parents have a poor experience of either health or education services themselves and may feel remote or disenchanted with 'the system'. Some may not be literate or have the confidence to talk to practitioners as an equal. Others may have limited social skills which make it hard for them to talk freely or form relationships easily.

Another group of parents may well be confident and literate in their home language but have only an elementary grasp of English which prevents them from becoming fully engaged with their child's education. Cultural issues can also affect how a parent deals with both their child's needs and with practitioners and professionals they come into contact with.

Having a child with special/additional needs inevitably affects how parents see themselves. We have already discussed the huge range of emotions experienced by parents and this can sometimes be exacerbated by the reactions of their family, friends and the wider community. Some relatives and friends are embarrassed and shy away from making contact while others may seem to feel sorry for or patronise them. Many parents feel that they are blamed or being judged for their child's difficulties.

It can be for all these reasons that many parents feel isolated, alone or as if nobody understands their situation.

# Factors to Consider When Working with Parents and Families

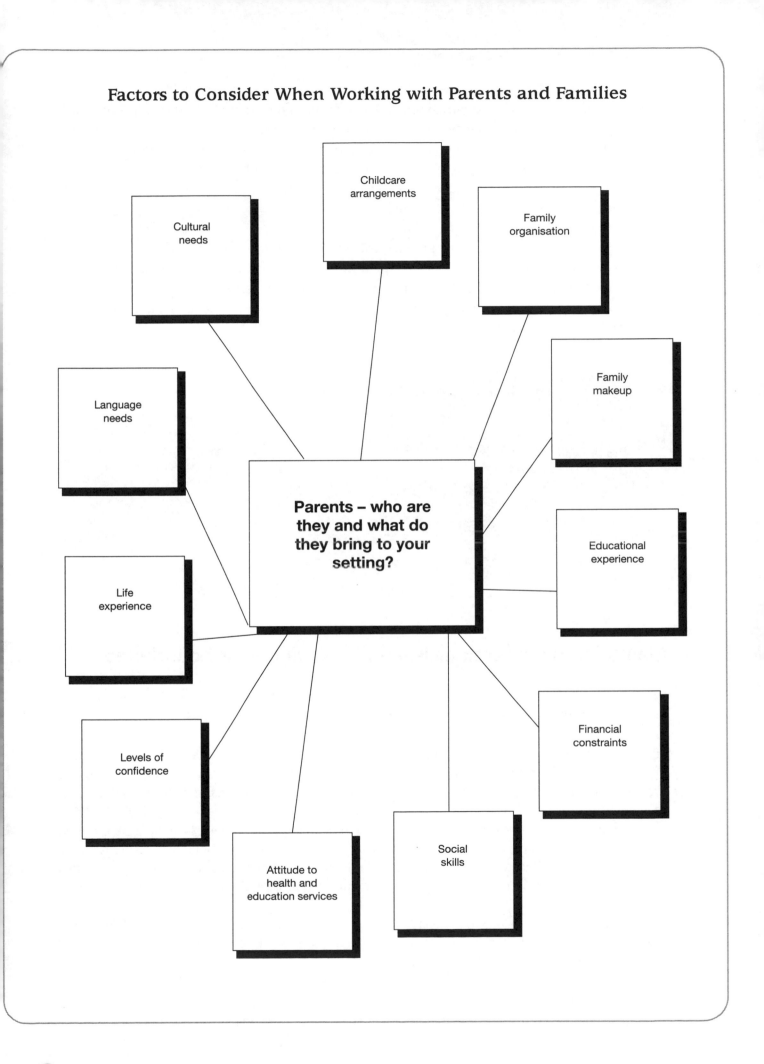

Childcare arrangements

Cultural needs

Family organisation

Language needs

Family makeup

**Parents – who are they and what do they bring to your setting?**

Educational experience

Life experience

Levels of confidence

Financial constraints

Attitude to health and education services

Social skills

Alongside all of this it is important to remember that, even though their child is still very young, many parents have already undertaken a long journey. They may have attended hospitals and seen countless professionals, and alongside coping with these practicalities they have had to deal with their own feelings and emotions. Some parents describe this process as being like a battle and for this reason they can sometimes appear to 'come out fighting' as they struggle to do the best they possibly can for their child.

This will continue to be an ongoing journey which will raise new issues and emotions at various points and milestones in their child's life. The role of the practitioner is to try to understand the needs of each parent, as well as their child, in order to find the best way of working together. At times this can be very challenging but the rewards of a successful partnership are invaluable for parent, practitioner and child.

 **Hands-on activity**

Consider one or two of the factors described such as:

❱ having to attend numerous hospital appointments with the child;

❱ being a lone parent of a child with significant special/additional needs.

Discuss how these may affect how a parent works with you in your pre-school.

## Maintaining professionalism and knowing your boundaries

Working closely with parents and children with special/additional needs, while offering challenges for practitioners, is one of the most rewarding areas of professional life.

Supporting children and parents through often difficult times ensures that a close bond develops between practitioner and the child's family. Outside of the family group, an effective practitioner is sometimes the only other adult who has a close relationship with the child.

All of the above adds to the professional satisfaction of many practitioners. However, there are no hard-and-fast rules on the type of relationship practitioners and parents should maintain. It is easy to fall into the role of trusted friend and support. Individual practitioners as well as setting managers need to make up their mind about how close a practitioner/family relationship should become.

When key working a child with special/additional needs it is recommended that regular meetings are held between key worker and SENCO or manager to share information and offer advice regarding situations that may arise.

Issues of confidentiality and 'need to know' as well as the remote possibility of child protection issues need to be considered in light of a close personal relationship between practitioner and parent/s.

# Maintaining Professionalism and Knowing Your Boundaries

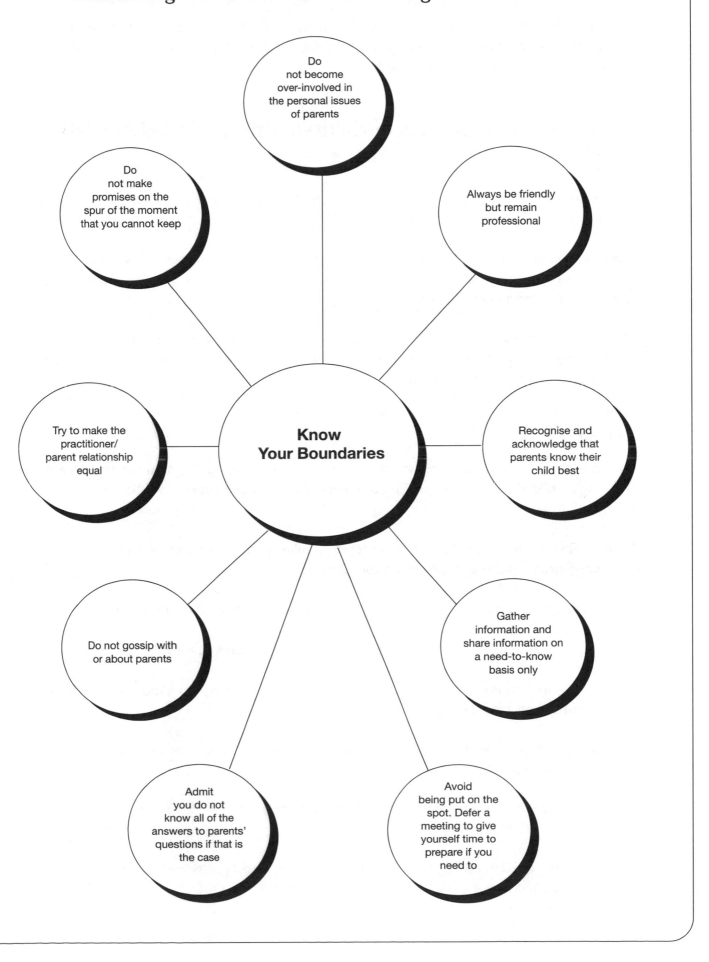

Do not become over-involved in the personal issues of parents

Do not make promises on the spur of the moment that you cannot keep

Always be friendly but remain professional

Try to make the practitioner/parent relationship equal

**Know Your Boundaries**

Recognise and acknowledge that parents know their child best

Do not gossip with or about parents

Gather information and share information on a need-to-know basis only

Admit you do not know all of the answers to parents' questions if that is the case

Avoid being put on the spot. Defer a meeting to give yourself time to prepare if you need to

The diagram on the preceding page 'Maintaining Professionalism and Knowing Your Boundaries' is intended to be used by key workers, SENCOs and managers as a prompt to discussing these issues within their settings.

# Reaching out to parents of children with special/additional needs

In our experience pre-schools lead the way in terms of positive parental relations. Practitioners realise and value the input of parents.

Time restraints for parents, frequent meetings with health professionals and stresses at home can sometimes put a strain on the parent/setting relationship, and occasionally misunderstandings and misinformation can occur.

Consider the strategies below that are helpful and easy to implement. By putting in place some or all of these suggestions you can be assured that you are doing your best to reach out to parents, even those who are harder to reach.

---

### Time

▶ Be flexible, especially when scheduling meetings. As a rule-of-thumb a meeting regarding a child should not occur without parents present (unless they give their permission for it to do so).

▶ Be flexible with regard to where meetings take place – sometimes it may be more appropriate to meet in the child's home.

▶ Always remind parents about meeting dates as some parents do not use a diary.

▶ Don't make yourself 100 per cent available but do tell parents when you can talk to them.

▶ Make sure parents have the time to talk to you; if not, rearrange to a more suitable time. A rushed meeting is generally not productive.

▶ Take the time to keep parents informed about how their child is doing (ways to do this are discussed in Chapter 5).

▶ Make sure you have enough time to do anything you tell parents you will do. Try not to make promises you can't keep.

▶ If parents need to bring younger children or babies to meetings with them either try to provide childcare or make sure there are toys and books for the child to play with in the meeting room.

---

## Value parents

▶ Try to welcome all parents daily.

▶ Learn a bit about parents such as their jobs, their interests and their abilities. It will give an extra dimension to the relationship.

▶ Learn about those cultural backgrounds different from your own – parents are often happy to give advice and information.

▶ Let parents know you value and trust their advice, recognise that they know their child best and be prepared to learn from them.

## Explain what you are doing and why you are doing it

▶ Work together to plan a settling-in period for their child.

▶ Inform parents if you have spoken to or heard from an outside professional who works with their child. (Note that, generally, parental permission is needed if the practitioner wants to talk to other professionals.)

▶ If a meeting needs to be cancelled due to time restraints, staff illness, etc. explain this to parents.

▶ If your routines need to be changed or if plans suddenly change, try to inform parents that this has happened.

## Help parents understand 'the system' (if they need to)

▶ Share information with parents about how things work, e.g. pre-school admissions, the key worker system, your area SENCO's role; and explain how you spend any monies received in grants, especially if they are given to help you include their child.

▶ Make sure parents know and understand the role of the key worker and SENCO in your setting. Sometimes parents don't realise that 'their' key worker may also key work several other children.

▶ Make sure parents have a copy of your relevant policies such as the settling-in policy and especially your SEN/inclusion policy.

▶ Parents need to know who they should go to when they need to discuss important issues regarding their child. That may be the setting manager, key worker or SENCO.

> **Support parents to participate**
>
> ▶ Always remember to ask parents their views in any meetings, especially those larger IEP meetings that may involve several professionals.
>
> ▶ Make sure that the parents' view is reflected in any IEP. (See Kate's case study below for an example of doing this.)
>
> ▶ Get into the habit of discussing home/school targets so parents are involved in their child's learning.
>
> ▶ Aim for a partnership approach with joint planning, evaluations, contributions, target setting, etc.
>
> ▶ Be a friend to parents but know your limitations (see the Maintaining Professionalism and Knowing Your Boundaries' diagram on page 66.)
>
> ▶ If parents are feeling overwhelmed help put them in touch with organisations that can support them. (See the list of contacts at the end of the book.)
>
> ▶ If any related training is offered to the setting to support a specific child, e.g. Makaton training, consider whether it would be appropriate to invite the child's parents to the training.
>
> ▶ Be prepared to learn from and with parents.

## Supporting parents with their children's learning: Individual Education Plans

Children who have special/additional needs are likely to have an Individual Education Plan (IEP) or an Individual Plan (IP).

Many parents are unfamiliar with these plans, an example of which has been included on page 73. It is important for parents to understand the purpose of an IEP or IP and how they can be involved in it.

The most obvious way to get parents involved is through the targets and activities themselves. Joint target-setting can strengthen relationships between parent and practitioner as well as proving hugely beneficial to the child. With their expert knowledge of their child parents have much to contribute to planning these targets. Practitioners need to recognise and listen to parent's suggestions and ideas and consider them alongside their own experience of the child, the setting and the curriculum.

Where joint targets are set for working on at home as well as at the pre-school, consideration should be given to targets which:

▶ are set within the context of everyday play and experiences at home;

▶ are not laboured, overdone or regarded as a chore;

▶ have variety and fun built in;

▶ take into account the interests of the child;

▶ are realistic in terms of what a parent is able to do in their individual circumstances, e.g. with regard to time, equipment;

▶ do not make parents or their child feel pressurised.

Some parents will feel more comfortable with the idea of joint targets than others for a variety of reasons. Practitioners should be sensitive to this and follow a few general rules:

▶ Avoid using jargon.

▶ Illustrate what you mean by giving a few examples of how a target could be worked on at home.

▶ Ask if parents have the toy, game or equipment needed.

▶ Offer to lend equipment or toys.

▶ Plan an opportunity for you to model a particular strategy while parents observe.

▶ Allow time for parents to ask questions and clarify any issues.

▶ Check how things are going after a week or so in case parents need further support.

An IEP gives information about the child and plans how the child can be supported. It includes:

▶ basic information;

▶ the child's strengths and difficulties;

▶ areas which need to be developed;

▶ specific targets for the child;

▶ what will be provided to help the child achieve the targets.

## Sharing skills parent/practitioner and practitioner/parent

 **Case Study**

### Kate

Kate is 3 years and 6 months and has recently been diagnosed with **developmental coordination and language difficulties**.

Her parents and health visitor became concerned when Kate was late in reaching her developmental milestones, especially those for physical and language and communication development.

Kate's parents have outlined her condition to the pre-school and welcomed a home visit.

A good relationship has been established between the pre-school staff, especially Kate's key worker and the pre-school SENCO and Kate's parents.

### Sharing skills – parents to practitioner – how Kate's parents shared their knowledge and skills with staff at the setting

Kate's parents have shared their understanding of Kate's condition with the pre-school by:

▶ Sharing all reports and information received from medical professionals.

▶ Inviting Kate's key worker to accompany them on a visit to the speech and language therapist to watch a session. (The key worker in return has invited the speech and language therapist to the pre-school.)

▶ Demonstrating to the key worker the speech and language exercises and games they do at home with Kate. These include looking at books together and using the pictures to retell the story.

▶ Showing the key worker they way they are teaching Kate to dress herself in the morning. This involves breaking down simple tasks such as rolling up a sock for Kate, placing it on her toes and letting her pull it up herself, as well as a technique for putting on a coat that involves Kate placing her coat on the floor in front of her, putting her arms through and then raising her arms to put the coat over her head.

▶ Introducing some of the home activities recommended by their physiotherapist. These activities are to help Kate to develop her fine motor control and include using inset jigsaws with handles and rolling play dough with two hands. They have even sent some of the activities to the pre-school so that Kate can show the staff how she manages.

## Sharing skills: practitioners to parents – how the setting staff shared their skills and knowledge with Kate's parents

▶ Through promoting shared home/school targets and activities (*see Kate's case study above*). For example, every week Sarah's key worker devises some activities that she will undertake with Sarah. She shares these with Sarah's parents and sends home a selection for Sarah to practise at home. These have included such things as cutting play dough with training scissors, practising buttoning, opening and closing jars and paper-folding activities.

▶ Sarah, Kate's key worker, noticed that Kate can succeed at activities and seems to learn better if the activity is broken down into easy steps with Sarah practising one step at a time. The key worker has modelled this technique to Kate's mother so she can do the same at home.

▶ Kate's key worker realised that by allowing Kate to finish off activities she was providing an opportunity to raise Kate's self-esteem and confidence. The key worker now uses a strategy that allows Kate to receive the satisfaction of finishing the activity, even if she has received a lot of support to carry out the task, e.g putting in the final piece of the jigsaw puzzle, threading the last bead, picking up the last piece of equipment during tidy-up time, putting the final piece of cutlery on the table, etc. She has shared this observation and technique with Kate's parents who try to do the same at home.

On the following pages is a completed sample copy of Kate's Individual Education Plan (IEP). The IEP reflects the shared target-setting and joint work undertaken by Kate's parents at home and the staff at the pre-school setting.

A useful parent information leaflet 'Let's talk About … Individual Plans or Individual Education Plans' is included at the end of the chapter.

The child benefits as their parent/carers are working in partnership with their key worker and SENCO. Skills are shared and the child benefits

Parents/carers have skills and knowledge in relation to their child. They share this information with the practitioner

# Sharing Skills

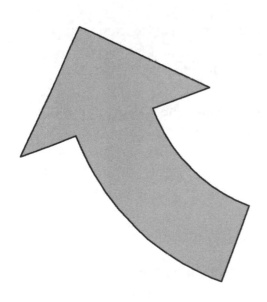

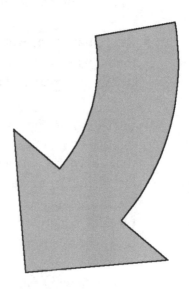

A practitioner has skills and knowledge about the early years curriculum and differentiation. With parental input they plan for the child

# Sample Individual Education Plan

| INDIVIDUAL EDUCATION PLAN No...1... | EYA / EYA+ / ST |
|---|---|
| Child's Name: *Kate Smiles* | D.O.B. *6.6.04* |

| Targets Set     Date: *October '06* | Review     Date: *February '07* |
|---|---|
| Target 1. *Kate will retell a simple story using picture clues.* <br><br> Action / Strategies *Share a simple story with Kate pointing at the pictures as you speak then ask Kate to read it to you, or her teddy or another child.* <br> By Whom *The same book will be used both at home and at pre-school. Kate will select a book and take it back and forward between pre-school and home for up to a week.* | Achieved? *Yes* <br> What has / has not been successful? *Kate has been working hard on this target by looking at a simple story book a week both at home and at pre-school. She especially likes to reread 'We're Going on a Bear Hunt'.* |
| Target 2. *Kate will complete a 6-piece inset puzzle independently* <br><br> Action / Strategies / Resources *Kate will take home a variety of fine motor activities at the weekend from pre-school. These will be some of the activities she has tried at pre-school.* <br><br> By whom *Key worker Sarah and Kate's parents. Coordinated by SENCO.* | Achieved? *Needs to be consolidated* <br><br> What has / has not been successful? *Kate sometimes finds puzzles frustrating as she only likes to use the type of puzzle with a handle; these have been hard to find.* |
| Target 3. *Kate will put on her outdoor shoes and coat by herself when going outside (weather permitting).* <br><br> Action / Strategies / Resources *All staff will support Kate to use the method she uses at home to put her coat on. Kate will be given extra time to put her coat on and a chair to sit on when putting her shoes on. Staff will ensure her shoes are on the right feet.* <br> By Whom *All setting staff and at home with parents.* | Achieved? *Yes* <br> What has / has not been successful? *Kate has loved showing her friends her technique for putting her coat on. All of the children are now using this method. Kate find finds her slip-on shoes easy but her shoes with the buckle are more difficult and staff support her when she wears these.* |

# Let's Talk About ...

## Individual Plans (IPs) or Individual Education Plans (IEPs)

Q. *What is an Individual Plan or Individual Education plan?*

A. These are both types of plan written for individual children who may have additional needs, in order to help them make progress.

The plan:

▶ will record information about the child;

▶ will record their strengths and the things that motivate them;

▶ will record the areas in which they need some help;

▶ will set specific targets for the child to work towards;

▶ will detail the support, resources and strategies which will be used to help them achieve those targets;

▶ will be reviewed regularly (usually once a term) to see what progress has been made and to set new targets.

Q. *Who decides what targets should be set?*

A. The targets will be set during discussions at an IP or IEP meeting which is usually held at the early years setting. You, as parents, as well as practitioners and anybody working with your child such as speech therapists or physiotherapists, will be asked to suggest suitable targets.

Q. *Are these targets the only thing my child will be working on at nursery?*

A. Your child will be doing all the usual nursery activities and the targets will be incorporated into the nursery planning. Sometimes it may be appropriate for some individual or small group time to be allocated when staff can work more specifically on targets with your child.

Q. *How will I be involved?*

A. You can be involved by:

▶ working on and practising the targets at home;

▶ attending the IP or IEP meetings;

▶ giving your views on how your child is progressing towards their targets;

▶ making suggestions for what they may need to work on next;

▶ liaising with the professionals involved with your child to make sure they contribute and give advice as well.

Working with Parents of Children with Special Educational Needs, Paul Chapman Publishing © Chris Dukes and Maggie Smith, 2007

**Further reading**

Department for Education and Skills (2003) *The Impact of Parents' Involvement on Children's Learning*. DfES.

Department for Education and Skills (2005) *Foundation Stage Parents: Partners in Learning*. DfES.

Department for Education and Skills (2006) *Special Educational Needs in Mainstream School: A Guide for the Beginner Teacher*. DfES.

CHAPTER FIVE

# It's good to talk: communicating with parents and professionals

The aim of this chapter is to help you develop positive methods of communicating with the parents of children in your setting with additional/special needs.

It focuses mainly on the pre-school SENCO whose role is central to building the links between parents, practitioners and other professionals.

It contains some useful pro-formas, top tips and helpful case studies.

This chapter also sets out guidance on:

▶ The role of the SENCO

▶ Supporting other members of staff

▶ Communicating with parents

▶ How to run effective meetings with parents

▶ Communicating with other professionals

▶ A guide to the roles of other professionals

## The role of the Special Educational Needs Coordinator (SENCO) or Inclusion Coordinator (INCO)

Every parent has a unique personality, beliefs and set of circumstances which will determine how they support their child and form a working relationship with practitioners.

The Special Educational Needs Code of Practice (DfES, 2001) suggests that it is the role of practitioners and professionals to support and empower parents to:

▶ recognise and fulfil their responsibilities as parents and play an active and valued role in their child's education;

▶ have knowledge of their child's entitlement within the SEN framework;

▶ make their views known about how their child is educated;

▶ have access to information, advice and support during assessment and any related decision-making processes about special educational provision.

The person most likely to take the lead in providing this support in an early years setting is the Special Educational Needs or Inclusion Coordinator (SENCO). The SENCO role is one which carries a great deal of responsibility, and careful thought needs to be given to who, in the pre-school, is best placed to fulfil that role.

The SENCO is responsible for:

▶ the *day-to-day organisation* and running of provision for children with special or additional needs;

▶ *record-keeping* – making sure that relevant background information about individual children is collected, recorded and updated;

▶ *advising* – supporting other practitioners in the setting;

▶ *planning* – helping to plan support for individuals in discussion with colleagues;

▶ *documenting* – ensuring that appropriate Individual Education Plans are in place and being carried out;

▶ *monitoring* – through observation and reviewing any actions or plans;

▶ *liaising* – creating links and dialogue between parents and other professionals in respect of children with special educational needs.

## Communicating with staff and parents

It is important that parents are aware of the SENCO role and that there is a clear procedure and guidelines for parents to follow if they need to discuss their child either before or while they attend your pre-school.

There are some very simple ways in which this can be done:

Have a space on the setting notice board which displays:

▶ your name and/or photograph;

▶ an outline of your role;

▶ what to do if parents are concerned about their child's development or learning;

▶ your setting's Special Needs or Inclusion Policy;

▶ details of any support services who visit your setting;

▶ contact details for local parent support groups.

It is also important that staff teams have a clear and realistic idea of the SENCO's role and how it operates in your setting.

Plan a training session for your staff team on:

▶ the role of the early years SENCO;

▶ how this applies in your own setting;

▶ your setting's Special Needs or Inclusion Policy;

▶ the responsibilities of individual staff members in working with parents of children with special/additional needs.

 **Hands-on activity**

**For the Pre-school setting SENCO**

Using the ideas mentioned above plan a Special Needs notice board for display in the entrance area of your setting.

# Supporting other members of staff to work with parents

## The importance of key workers

It is important that all staff are aware of their own responsibilities for working with all parents, especially those whose children have special/additional needs. The Code of Practice makes it clear that **all** staff are responsible for working with and supporting children with special or additional needs. This includes observing, planning and delivering individualised programmes.

Key workers who have responsibility for working with a child on a daily basis are in a unique position to work with parents. Not only have they got

to know an individual child but they also have broader experience of a range of children and their needs, a knowledge of child development and a wealth of ideas and strategies for play and the curriculum.

Ideally the first port of call for any parent who has concerns about their child should always be the child's key worker. By the same token, any concerns that staff may have should also initially be raised with parents by the key worker. This, however, is not always as straightforward as it sounds and sometimes there are barriers to even the first steps to working with parents.

These barriers can include **parents**:

▶ not having a positive or perhaps any relationship with their child's key worker;

▶ not feeling confident to talk about their child's needs or difficulties;

▶ feeling that they are being blamed or judged because of their child's needs;

▶ lacking understanding of their child's needs;

▶ lacking knowledge about their child's particular special/additional need;

◗ not acknowledging their child's needs or difficulties;

◗ feeling unsupported in trying to meet their child's needs;

◗ having concern that things are being taken out of their hands;

◗ feeling that their opinions are not heard or valued.

These barriers can also include **key workers**:

◗ not having a positive or perhaps any relationship with parents;

◗ not feeling confident to talk about more difficult topics with parents;

◗ having a negative attitude to parents, e.g. seeing the parents as part of the 'problem';

◗ lacking understanding of a child's needs;

◗ lacking knowledge of a particular special/additional need;

◗ having a negative or inflexible attitude to meeting individual needs;

◗ feeling unsupported in trying to meet a child's needs.

## Issues and ideas for managers and SENCOs to reflect upon

Each setting and staff team must find its own way forward but it is the role of the SENCO to take the lead in trying to break down some of these barriers and address the underlying issues. This can be done only with the support of other staff, and the manager in particular has a key role to play. It should be remembered that the manager/owner is ultimately responsible for ensuring that all aspects of a pre-school, including building relationships with parents and meeting individual children's needs, are provided to a satisfactory standard. It may be worth considering some of the following:

*Staff are able to support parents better if they themselves feel supported so*:

◗ have regular slots at staff meetings where colleagues can raise concerns or discuss individual children;

◗ offer support to colleagues by spending some time in each room or group within your setting, talking to staff and observing children;

◗ when there are resources available release staff to carry out their focused observations, write IEPs or meet with parents, etc.;

▶ meet with parents alongside key workers;

▶ organise training on particular special needs or conditions as well as wider issues of inclusion. This will encourage discussion, broaden staff knowledge and increase confidence.

*If staff have a good supportive relationship with parents, difficult issues are more easily approached so*:

▶ be flexible when allocating key workers – if the child and/or parent makes a bond with a particular member of staff consider changing the key worker to accommodate this.

▶ create opportunities for key workers and parents to meet more informally to build up relationships. This can be during workshops, coffee mornings, volunteer helper sessions, trips, etc.;

▶ act as the 'parent voice' – sometimes it is invaluable to remind colleagues of how a parent might be feeling and encourage them to put themselves in a parent's shoes.

*Have practical procedures in place which will support your policy of working with parents*:

▶ have clear methods of communicating and exchanging information between key workers, SENCO and parents;

▶ have well-organised arrangements for informal and more formal meetings, which take into account parents' individual circumstances;

▶ offer to support parents at meetings with other professionals;

▶ create opportunities for joint working through everyday activities as well as Individual Plans (IPs) or Individual Education Plans (IEPs).

These practical issues will be explored in more detail over following pages as we look at methods of communication and meetings with parents.

# Communicating with parents

Just as every parent needs to be treated as an individual so the methods of communicating with each parent need to be tailored to their particular needs and circumstances.

While some parents bring their children into nursery every day, others are seen only on the odd occasion, so reaching out to all parents can be a challenge.

For example, research has shown how important a role fathers play in their children's lives and that a father's involvement is significantly related to positive outcomes for a child. Yet the term 'parent' itself is often perceived as meaning mother, leaving fathers all but forgotten.

While it can be a sensitive area, with issues around non-resident fathers or parental responsibility, it is an important question to address at your setting, particularly when a child has a special or additional need. Staff need to feel comfortable about welcoming fathers, to emphasise their role, stress the benefits for their children and make efforts to target activities which encourage involvement.

Those families who have English as an additional language and whose children have a special educational need are also likely to need more creative approaches to staying in contact. Using family members who can translate is sometimes the best way to overcome any language barriers. Care should be taken, however, especially if older children are translators, and for some parents there are also issues around privacy and confidentiality when either immediate family or friends are helping in this way. Practitioners should be sensitive to this and where possible seek advice from the local authority or community groups who may be able to provide independent translators.

It is often a good idea when parents first approach the nursery or during pre-admission visits to talk to parents about the best way of communicating with them. Nursery application forms usually have space for some contact details but do not always ask for a preferred method of communication or indeed give alternatives to a straightforward telephone call.

To working parents and families of children with special or additional needs who have particular pressures with appointments, hospital visits as well as their other commitments, effective communication is essential.

The following suggestions are just some of the ways by which settings can attempt to reach all parents.

## Ideas for communicating with parents

▶ *Pre-school prospectus*
   This outlines your values and ethos and it is particularly important to highlight your welcoming and inclusive policies and practice. It is sometimes useful to have it translated into the most popular community languages.

▶ *Parents' notice board*
   This is very useful for displaying current information about staff, routines and projects. However, not all parents drop off or collect children, some rush through without noticing and others have children who miss parts of the week, so weekly notices sent home can be a helpful backup.

▶ *Newsletters*
   A monthly newsletter can be extremely helpful for keeping parents in touch not only with what has been going on but also as a way of preparing for the weeks ahead. Asking for volunteers or contributions of various kinds can be done in advance which gives all parents a chance to rearrange schedules or work and means that you are more likely to involve a greater number of parents. It gives parents of children with special needs time to prepare their children for new experiences or changes in routines or to talk about themes or projects.

▶ *Home/pre-school diary (or boomerang book)*

This is particularly useful for individual children working towards targets or those who need extra support or encouragement. It can be helpful to highlight current interests, to give notice of changes in routine which can then be prepared for or to note concerns. Entries about the child should always focus on positive aspects and achievements.

▶ *Information leaflets or booklets*

These are a great way to let parents know about particular aspects of the curriculum and pre-school planning. They can give details about activities which will be taking place in the setting and the purpose and benefits of those activities. Ideas of how parents can support their child at home are always appreciated. Remember, however, to make sure that ideas are suitable for children with special or additional needs and that expectations are realistic.

▶ *Audio information*

Technology now enables information to be recorded and transmitted in many different forms. Tapes or CDs are an excellent way of reaching parents who perhaps are unable or reluctant to read but who would listen to information presented aurally. This can be done while driving or even doing the ironing!

▶ *A suggestion box*

This is a simple but effective way to encourage involvement, especially for those parents who wish to remain anonymous. Suggestions can be general or you can use it when you want opinions on a particular subject – anything from the snack menu to what the next pre-school outing should be. It can also provide a safe vehicle for parents to voice concerns or worries.

▶ *Parent helper rotas*

This is another way to involve parents in the day-to-day activities and get to know them a little better. Remember to discuss issues of confidentiality and health and safety with any volunteers in your setting.

A directory of parent skills is also useful and means you can ask both mothers and fathers to help on particular projects which you might otherwise not attempt. Having their parent in the setting for a session is often is a very positive experience for both children with special needs and the parent. Please note parents should always be supervised.

▶ *Information evenings*

Again this is a great way to pass on information, to give parents a chance to ask questions and to try out some activities for themselves. Differentiated activities should always be available and the steps towards goals explained. Active learning sessions and direct invitations appeal more to fathers!

▶ *Informal coffee mornings or social events*

Some parents may well be uncomfortable or intimidated by curriculum-based evenings but would be happier going to a social event. Traditional coffee mornings are often popular but also consider fish and chip suppers, cheese and wine evenings or barbecues to attract those who may not be free during the day. It can help staff get to know parents in a relaxed atmosphere but also helps parents network together which is very important for parents who may feel isolated.

▶ *Progress meetings/IEP reviews*
Many settings have termly progress meetings for all children. It is, however, very important to monitor the progress of those who have specific targets and needs. Regular meetings make sure that the child's needs are being met and that support is directed accordingly.

▶ *Photographs*
Every parent loves a photo of their child and this is a great way of showing achievement or progress towards a target when they are at nursery. Parents can also take pictures and send them in to show their child playing and learning at home. In this way joint target-setting and planning is easily possible.

▶ *Video clips*
These are extensions of the photographic evidence and give parents and practitioners a real insight into how a child functions at nursery and at home. Permission must be gained from all parents to photograph or video their child and other children.

▶ *E-mail or text message*
This can be very useful to busy parents who perhaps are at work or on the move. Some fathers particularly favour short and to-the-point messages which do not involve long conversations but convey the necessary information. A good addition to your admissions form would be a request for e-mail and mobile numbers and permission to use them as points of contact.

▶ *Telephone or mobile phone*
For many people the telephone is the next best thing to a face-to-face conversation. Important news or discussions should not, however, be carried out over the telephone. Reactions are difficult to judge without body language and facial expressions, so calls are best confined to making arrangements for a proper meeting.

## Hands-on activity

How do you communicate with parents in your setting?

Are there some parents you find hard to reach?

Use the suggestions to help you to identify some ways in which you could improve communication. Draw up a short action plan.

# Communicating with parents

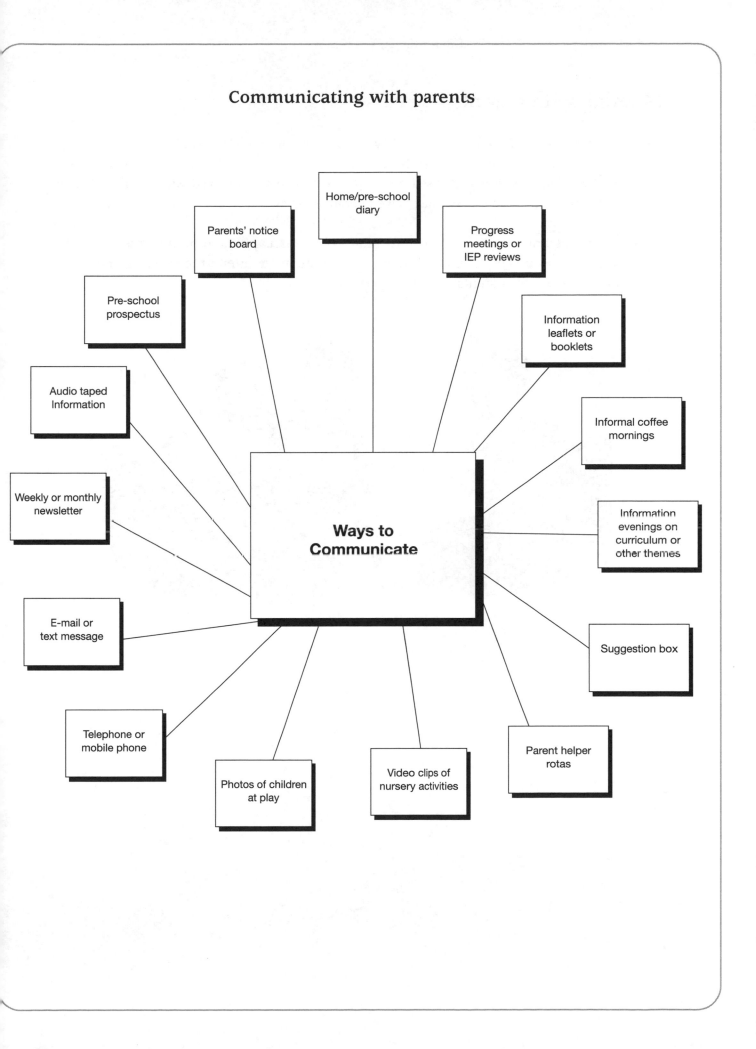

**Ways to Communicate**

- Home/pre-school diary
- Parents' notice board
- Progress meetings or IEP reviews
- Pre-school prospectus
- Information leaflets or booklets
- Audio taped Information
- Informal coffee mornings
- Weekly or monthly newsletter
- Information evenings on curriculum or other themes
- E-mail or text message
- Suggestion box
- Telephone or mobile phone
- Parent helper rotas
- Photos of children at play
- Video clips of nursery activities

# Meeting with parents

Meetings can be one of the most stressful events not only for parents but also for practitioners. There are some very simple ways that these stresses can be reduced by careful preparation and thought. A well planned and organised meeting leaves everyone involved with a sense of satisfaction even when more difficult issues have been discussed.

On the following pages are some useful tips for both preparing for and running meetings with parents, as well as a sample letter of invitation to parents, to attend the meeting and a proforma prompt sheet for parents' use during the meetings.

# 10 Tips for
# Preparing for Meetings with Parents

1. Ask parents when the most convenient days and times for meetings might be before you make any arrangements.

2. Make sure you give enough notice of meetings to allow parents to prepare and organise time off work or childcare. A note or written reminder is often appreciated a week or a few days before the meeting.

3. Encourage parents to bring a friend or relative with them if they feel they need support.

4. Be specific about the purpose of the meeting so that parents know what to expect. It is helpful to have an agenda which is given to parents in advance.

5. Encourage parents to think about what they might like to say or talk about at the meeting.

6. Make sure parents are aware of who else will be at the meeting so they are not suddenly confronted with a whole group of professionals. Ask parents if there is any body else they would like to attend.

7. If you would like parents to bring any reports or information, ask them if this is possible and offer to photocopy the documents for them if necessary.

8. Make sure you have all the information you need to hand, such as progress towards IEP targets, recent successes, observations, etc. Complete the administrative parts of any forms such as names, date of birth, etc. beforehand.

9. Organise a private meeting space, chairs, tables, water, etc.

10. Decide who will chair the meeting and who will take notes – it is very difficult to do both.

# 10 Tips for
# Meetings with Parents

1. Make sure that you either introduce every body or ask people to introduce themselves.

2. Be sensitive to how parents might be feeling and use the knowledge and relationship you already have with them to put them at ease.

3. Ask if there are any objections to notes being taken and indicate that all those present will be given copies of those notes.

4. Try not to ask for parents' contributions first, as being the first to speak at a meeting is always quite hard.

5. Make sure that parents have the chance to comment on the views of the other people present.

6. Always start with the positives for a child like progress and successes. Avoid using jargon and clarify any terminology that may be used.

7. Offer time to have a break or a drink if at any point parents seem to be stressed or upset, so that they can gather their thoughts.

8. Keep to time by remaining focused and arrange another time to meet if there are additional matters to be discussed which have not been planned for. It can be difficult for parents who may need to return to work or pick up other children if a meeting overruns.

9. Summarise the outcomes of the meeting so that everyone is clear as to what has been agreed. If possible circulate any notes or IEPs etc. immediately; if not, make sure you have contact details in order to send them later.

10. Set a date for the next meeting while everyone is present.

 Working with Parents of Children with Special Educational Needs, Paul Chapman Publishing © Chris Dukes and Maggie Smith, 2007

# Sample Letter of Invitation

Smiley Faces Nursery
Grinning Lane
Laughvale

1st January 2007

Dear Parent

As discussed earlier we would like to invite you to / remind you about a

meeting on _____ at _____

The meeting is being held to discuss _____

_____

Also attending the meeting will be _____

_____

We attach a Parents' Meeting sheet and hope that it is helpful to you in preparing for the meeting. Please contact us if you have any questions or suggestions.

We look forward to seeing you.

Best wishes

Ms Smiley

# Meeting Prompt Sheet for Parents

Date of meeting _____ Time_____

Things I need to take with me

E.g. reports

What I would like to say

Issues I would like to raise / discuss

Outcomes / Actions agreed / Things to do

Other notes

**Date / time of next meeting**

# Practitioners Record a Meeting with Parents

| Record of meeting with parents | Date: |
|---|---|

**Child's name:**                                         **D.O.B.**

**Present at meeting:**

**Reason for the meeting:**

**Information / what was discussed:**

**What should happen next:**

Working with Parents of Children with Special Educational Needs, Paul Chapman Publishing © Chris Dukes and Maggie Smith, 2007

## Communicating with other professionals

It is very important to try and liaise with any professional who works with a child in your pre-school. Children's needs are often slightly different in a pre-school setting than they might be at home and practitioners sometimes have different questions and queries from parents regarding individual children.

Communicating with professionals from outside your own pre-school can be of huge benefit to the child but it can also be a frustrating and time-consuming task for you to reach the person you need when you need them. Most professionals welcome dialogue with practitioners, and difficulties in communicating are largely due to the heavy work and case loads which most professionals have, rather than any unwillingness to share information.

Some 'Top Tips' follow to help you start building the basis for good working relationships, and a list of some professionals you may meet along the way, with a brief description of their roles.

What do I want to know
or need help with?

Who is the best person
to help me or give me
the information I need?

When will I next
review progress
and contact the
professional
again?

Talking
to Outside
Professionals
about a Child

Have I got the parents'
permission to talk to
the professional
concerned?

How will I record the
information and pass it
on to colleagues?

Do I have all the
relevant contact details
for the professional?

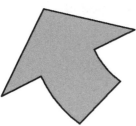

# Top Tips for
# Communicating with Professionals

▶ Remember that any discussions with outside professionals must be done with the knowledge and consent of parents.

▶ If you have a regular group of professionals who work with your setting make sure that they are introduced on your notice board and in your prospectus.

▶ Ask parents to help you compile a list of all the professionals involved with their child.

▶ List their contact details – this makes it easier when arranging meetings and sending letters.

▶ List days and working hours so you don't waste time ringing on a day they are not at work.

▶ Ask them their preferred method of communication – e-mails are often convenient for quick enquiries if the person is office-based.

▶ Prepare a list of questions or information you would like before you speak to them. This will help to keep the conversation focused and ensure that you don't forget the point of your call.

▶ Give at least 4–6 weeks' notice of any meeting you would like them to attend.

▶ Ask for some written feedback or suggestions for IEP targets if they are unable to attend your meeting.

▶ Send copies of any relevant documents, such as IEPs, to them to keep them informed of what is happening. This also encourages them to do the same.

▶ Ask to be put on the circulation list for reports etc. Make sure parents are in agreement with this.

▶ Keep a record of all contacts, including telephone calls and e-mails, with a brief note of what was discussed.

▶ Look at the record before you make your next contact to remind you of what was discussed last time.

▶ Try to make contact on a regular basis even if it's just to get an update on progress. This helps to build firmer relationships.

▶ Don't forget to tell parents and colleagues that you have been in touch with an outside professional and let them know what you discussed.

 *Working with Parents of Children with Special Educational Needs, Paul Chapman Publishing © Chris Dukes and Maggie Smith, 2007*

# Record of Professionals Involved with a Child

| Child's name: | Date of birth: |
|---|---|
| Name | Position |
| Address | Working days / hours |
| | |
| Telephone | E-mail |
| Name | Position |
| Address | Working days / hours |
| | |
| Telephone | E-mail |
| Name | Position |
| Address | Working days / hours |
| | |
| Telephone | E-mail |
| Name | Position |
| Address | Working days / hours |
| | |
| Telephone | E-mail |

## Professionals and their roles

Local authorities, both health and education services and early years development and child-care partnerships (EYDCPs) have a range of services to support pre-school settings and parents. These may include:

▶ *Portage worker*

Portage is a home teaching service. It works with children who have special needs aged 0–5 years and their families. Portage workers visit children in their homes on a regular basis to assess and teach new skills. They model the teaching of each skill to enable parents and carers to work with their child in between visits. In this way parents and workers are able to work together, pool their knowledge of the child and support each other. Many authorities have Portage workers or those who carry out a similar role.

▶ *Educational psychologist*

An educational psychologist provides specialist assessment of all kinds of learning difficulties. They can give advice on teaching and management strategies and behaviour management. They will always become involved if a child is having a statutory assessment.

▶ *Clinical psychologist*

Clinical psychologists work within health service settings. They provide individual and family counselling, family therapy and advice. They can advise on and provide support for a variety of issues including behaviour management and conditions such as autism.

▶ *Speech and language therapist*

Speech and language therapists will assess, give advice to families and work directly with children who have a speech, language or communication disorder. They also work with children who have related eating and swallowing difficulties, giving advice on feeding, sucking, food, and mouth and tongue movement.

▶ *Physiotherapist*

Physiotherapists work mainly with children with physical difficulties or delay. They give advice and support and plan individual programmes which centre on issues such as exercise, coordination and balance. They will also advise on specialist equipment like splints, braces, wheelchairs and buggies.

▶ *Occupational therapist*

Occupational therapists work with children who need help in developing practical life skills because of some form of physical, psychological or social delay or disability. They provide advice and access to specialised equipment both at home and in the pre-school, such as chairs, bathing or toileting aids and adaptations to everyday items.

▶ *Community doctors and paediatricians*

Doctors and paediatricians work alongside parents to identify and diagnose various illnesses or conditions. They monitor medical conditions as the child grows older and can also refer to other health service professionals.

▶ *Health visitors*

Every pre-school child has a health visitor allocated through their local GP. Health visitors will visit families at home when a child is born and they also run various clinics for immunisations, sleep and general development checks. They are available for help, support and advice on all development and health issues.

▶ *Social workers*

Social workers support children and families in difficult circumstances. They can provide advice and access to other social services provision such as respite care. They will also become involved when there are child protection issues or procedures in place.

▶ *Curriculum adviser*

These are teachers who can give advice and support on curriculum and planning issues. They will advise on general good practice throughout the pre-school.

▶ *The pre-school Learning Alliance*

While this organisation is not run by local authorities it often works closely with EYDCPs. The workers are experienced practitioners with a wide range of knowledge and expertise who can help, support and advise on a variety of issues.

▶ *Inclusion adviser/Area SENCO*

These are teachers or early years specialists who can advise on inclusion and working with children with special needs. They often have extensive experience or specialist qualifications in working with children with particular needs, such as hearing or visual impairments. Some are involved in direct teaching while others fulfil a more advisory role.

The following pro-forma is a good way of recording the contact details of the professionals involved with an individual child and can be compiled with the help of parents. This makes arranging meetings and sending letters far easier. It is particularly useful for those children who do not have complex needs and so do not have this information collected together in Early Support Files, for example.

 **Hands-on activity**

Use the pro-forma to list the professionals involved with an individual child in your setting.

Begin to create a 'Directory of Professionals'.

**Further reading**

Drifte, C. (2005) *A Manual for the Early Years SENCO*. Paul Chapman Educational.

Gorman, J. C. (2004) *Working with Challenging Parents of Students with Special Needs*. Corwin Press.

Mortimer, H. and McNicholas, S. (2004) *SEN Co-ordinator's Handbook* (Special Needs in the Early Years). Scholastic.

# CHAPTER SIX

# Scaffolding: supporting parents through challenging times

The aim of this chapter is to highlight some the issues facing the parents of children with special/additional needs at particular times. It gives ideas and strategies for supporting parents and their children through illness, diagnosis and the statutory assessment process.

This chapter sets out guidance on:

▶ Recognising parents' feelings

▶ Supporting parents when their child gets a diagnosis

▶ Working with parents when their child has medical needs

▶ When a child is ill or in hospital

▶ Children with complex needs

▶ The statutory assessment procedures

▶ Common conditions and difficulties

Parents can feel a huge range of emotions when they discover that their child may have a special need or a disability. Some of these feelings are highlighted in the diagram on page 102.

There are no rules as to how parents may feel and each person experiences and copes with the news in their own way. Indeed, where there are two parents, each of them may have very different views and feelings.

As parents live with the reality of caring for and bringing up a child with a special/additional need, feelings change, adapt and re-emerge. At times it can be what some parents have described as an emotional rollercoaster.

This can put a tremendous strain on individual parents and their relationships, and research has shown that a higher proportion of marriages or partnerships fail as a result of the pressures that they feel under.

Practitioners are not always in a position to help parents deal with their feelings. They are, however, in a position to welcome and support their children. This in itself is a great support to parents and there is often a huge sense of relief when they realise that they are not alone. They have someone who is interested in their child's needs and how they can be met and are willing to work alongside them to help their child reach their potential.

# Feelings Parents may Experience

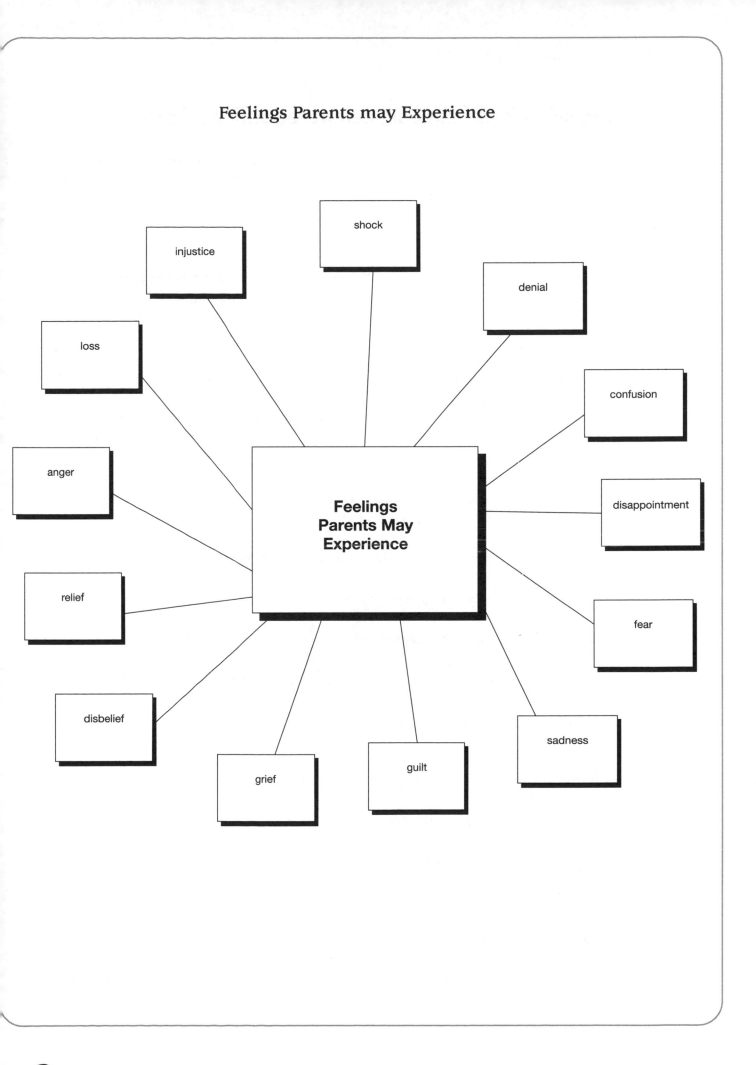

# How pre-schools can support parents at difficult times

There are some times which cause parents particular anxiety, stress or upset. It is at these times that practitioners need to be most supportive and understanding. A few of these occasions are outlined on the following pages along with some ideas of how practitioners can help.

## Diagnosis

Many parents find receiving a diagnosis helpful because it finally gives a name to their child's difficulties. This can help parents understand their child's needs and difficulties and can motivate them to seek further help and support for both themselves and their child. It can also be helpful in trying to explain them to others in the family or the wider social circle. A name or diagnosis can also sometimes prepare parents for what may lie ahead in terms of their child's development and future needs.

For other parents, however, their child having a diagnosis is a less than positive experience. The negative connotations of a child being 'labelled', particularly at an early age, can change the way parents see their child, their child's abilities and future progress.

Parents will undoubtedly experience a range of emotions and many are very vulnerable at this time, whatever their attitude to receiving a diagnosis.

▶ Do not make any presumptions about how parents might be feeling.

▶ Allow time for parents to let a diagnosis sink in.

▶ Avoid bombarding them with questions or asking them to make decisions.

▶ Do some general research so you have a basic knowledge of their child's condition.

▶ Invite parents to come, when they are ready, and discuss how their child can best be supported.

▶ Have information available on parent support groups in your area.

▶ Avoid overloading them with information.

▶ Find some joint targets to work on at home as well as in the pre-school.

▶ Make sure that you liaise with the appropriate professionals to get advice.

▶ Meet regularly and keep parents informed of progress.

▶ Remember that parents need ongoing support as their child reaches different ages and stages.

▌ Remember to be sensitive to how parents *might* be feeling in relation to other parents or children at your setting.

▌ Remember that the child is still the same child whatever their diagnosis.

▌ Focus on the child's strengths as well as areas of need.

▌ Working together has the best results for a child but trust has to be earned.

 **Hands-on activity**

What might parents who have recently received a diagnosis for their child find difficult when coming to the nursery each day? Continue the list below.

▌ Answering questions about the future

▌ Staff treating them differently

▌

# Working with parents of children with medical needs and health care plans

Most children at some time will have short-term medical needs such as finishing a course of antibiotics; others have needs at particular times such as an allergic reaction or hay fever, while a smaller group will have long-term medical needs to keep them healthy.

Children with medical needs have the same rights of admission to settings as any other child and the duties of early years settings under the Disability Discrimination Act (DDA) 1995 includes children with medical needs as well as those with disabilities. All settings should consider supporting children with complex health needs and managing medicines as part of their accessibility planning duties.

While some children with medical or health needs will also have special educational needs it should be remembered, however, that 'a medical diagnosis or a disability does not *necessarily* imply a special educational need. It is the child's educational needs rather than a medical diagnosis that must be considered' (Special Educational Needs Code of Practice, 2001: para. 7.64–7.67).

The government has produced guidance entitled *Managing Medicines in Schools and Early Years Settings* (DfES/DoH, 2005). This guidance is designed to help schools and early years settings develop effective management systems to support individual children with medical needs who may also require access to their medicines while in school. It covers:

1. Developing medicines policies

2. Roles and responsibilities

3. Dealing with medicines safely

4. Drawing up a health care plan (including sample plans)

5. Common conditions – practical advice on asthma, epilepsy, diabetes and anaphylaxis.

Many local authorities also produce their own guidance in line with their own local services and organisation.

 **Hands-on activity**

What information do you think would be recorded on a Health Care Plan?
Continue the list below:

▶ The name of a child's doctor

▶ A health professional's signature

▶

Check your answer with the suggestions in *Managing Medicines in Schools and Early Years Settings* (DfES, 2005: Annex B, Page 44), or in local authority guidelines.

The guidance also recognises that 'If a child's medical needs are inadequately supported this may have a significant impact on a child's experiences and they way they function in or out of a school or setting' (DfES, 2005: Chapter 1, para. 38).

Although parents have prime responsibility for their child's health, they need to feel that their child is safe and that their well-being is paramount when they are away from home and attending an early years setting. Parents can sometimes appear to practitioners as being fussy or overprotective. Staff therefore need to work closely with parents to reassure them that they take their responsibilities towards the child seriously and to build up trust and confidence in the staff's ability to support the child.

In order to achieve this settings should ensure that:

▶ a child's needs are talked about before they are admitted to a setting in order that they can be planned for;

▶ medical advice and support is sought for each individual child and that parents provide information about their child's medical condition, needs and medicines. This should include information from appropriate professionals such as GPs, paediatricians or health visitors as necessary;

▶ a health care plan is in place for every child that needs one and that it is reviewed;

▶ confidentiality is respected – every child has the right for their health details to be kept confidential. Information should be on a need-to-know basis. In some instances it may be beneficial or in the child's interest to share information with other children and parents, e.g. in relation to a nut allergy, at the setting – this can be done only with parents' express permission and support;

▶ activities are discussed with parents to check that they are suitable and do not put the child at risk;

▶ support is provided for any activities as necessary;

▶ special and/or flexible arrangements can be made for individual children's needs such as those who attend hospital appointments on a regular basis;

▶ staff access appropriate training and support from health professionals – in every area there should be access to training from local health services and for children under 5 the responsibility lies with health visitors;

▶ staff are not put at risk or into situations they are not confident and/or trained to deal with;

▶ dialogue is maintained with parents to ensure information is up to date.

 **Hands-on activity**

What information and preparations might you need to make for a child with complex medical needs when planning:

(a) a trip or educational visit?

(b) sporting activities?

# Supporting parents when their child is ill or in hospital

Some children with special/additional needs may find themselves having sometimes lengthy absences through illness or hospitalisation. This can be a worrying time for both children and their families. Grandparents, siblings and friends as well as parents are affected by a child being unwell or away from home.

It is important to try to support parents at this time as well as to realise that they can be under particular strain. Many will be trying to continue working or juggling a job, looking after other children and running a home while caring for a sick child at home or making frequent visits to hospital. Perhaps either one or both parents may well be staying at the hospital with their child if required.

All of this makes for exhausted parents who can feel very isolated as so much of their time is taken up with day-to-day arrangements they have little spare time to see friends and other family members.

There are ways that you can support parents before a child goes into hospital, for example by reading books about going into hospital with all the children or setting up doctors' surgeries for role-play activities.

You should, however, check with the parents concerned before planning any activity of this sort as there may be issues around confidentiality. You should also be prepared for any questions which children or other adults might raise as a result of any discussion or the knowledge that a child is unwell or going into hospital.

Hospitals also now have a variety of leaflets for parents and children on various aspects of a hospital stay or particular conditions. Many too have websites which give similar information and have pages of Frequently Asked Questions (FAQs) designed for parents.

Encouraging parents to make the most of local support can also be helpful.

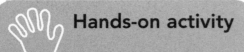

## Hands-on activity

What sort of questions would you have if your child was going into hospital?

Use the internet to find a local hospital website and gather some information about a hospital stay.

Maintaining a link between parents and pre-school at these times sends the clear message that you care about their child and are interested in how the whole family is feeling. This can be very reassuring to parents who worry about what their child may be missing out on and how they will settle back into nursery after their recovery.

Depending on individual circumstances and your relationship with the parents there are several relatively simple ways to ensure that you keep in touch and are also part of the child's world even though they are not attending the nursery. Some of these are in the diagram on the next page.

There is also a pro-forma on page 109 for keeping in touch with parents and exchanging news and information.

# Supporting Parents When Their Child Is Ill or in Hospital

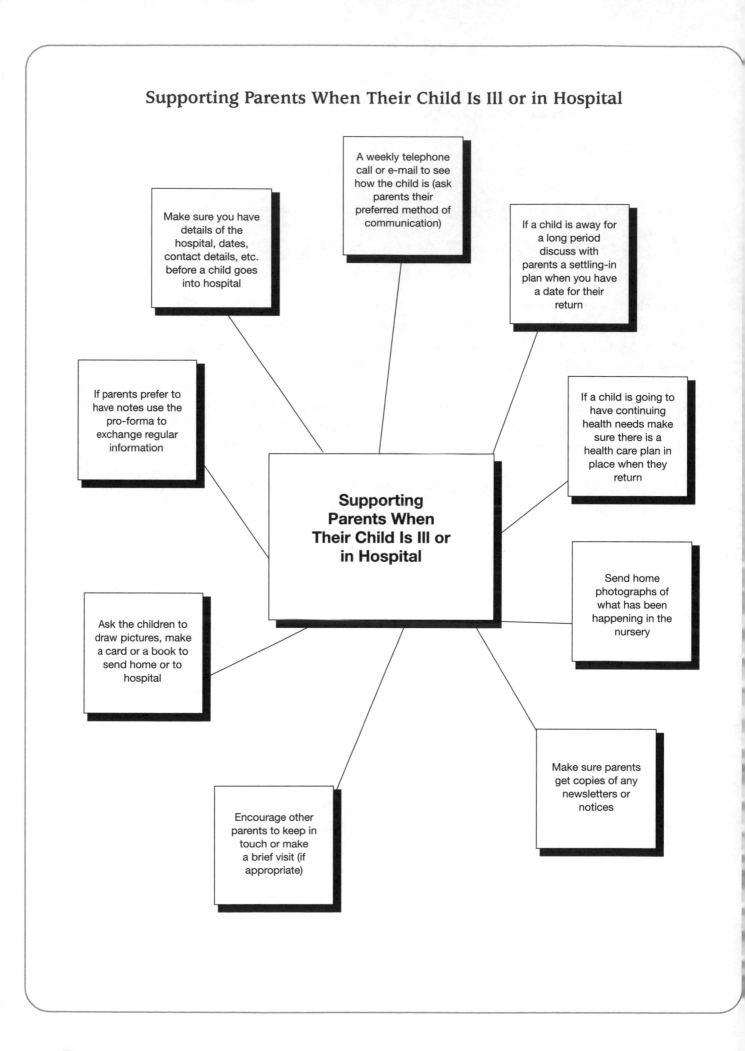

A weekly telephone call or e-mail to see how the child is (ask parents their preferred method of communication)

Make sure you have details of the hospital, dates, contact details, etc. before a child goes into hospital

If a child is away for a long period discuss with parents a settling-in plan when you have a date for their return

If parents prefer to have notes use the pro-forma to exchange regular information

If a child is going to have continuing health needs make sure there is a health care plan in place when they return

**Supporting Parents When Their Child Is Ill or in Hospital**

Send home photographs of what has been happening in the nursery

Ask the children to draw pictures, make a card or a book to send home or to hospital

Make sure parents get copies of any newsletters or notices

Encourage other parents to keep in touch or make a brief visit (if appropriate)

## Home - setting / Setting - Home Information

Week beginning _____

In the nursery this week we will be ...

At home this week we have ...

Health update / information / notes

# Working with families of children with complex needs

Children with complex needs and their families often have a whole range of needs in addition to those experienced by the majority of parents of children with special or additional needs.

*Together from the Start*, a document produced by the DfES in 2003 providing practical guidance for professionals working with disabled children and their families, recognises that:

> *Where children have special needs or disabilities, it is important that these are identified at an early stage and that identification leads directly to early intervention and support for families and children. It emphasises that early intervention strengthens the ability of families to provide effective support for their children and improves outcomes for the whole family.* (DfES, 2003: 5)

## The key principles for working with families

These include:

▶ Parents have rights and responsibilities in relation to the development and care of their child. Professionals have a duty to acknowledge and understand the unique role and relationship each parent has with their child.

▶ Parents have unique knowledge about their child and they have the right to be respected as the primary carers of their child.

▶ Parents have the right to be provided with unbiased, accurate and up-to-date information in order to be able to make informed and appropriate choices for their child.

▶ There are many common issues for parents of disabled children, but no two families are the same or have identical needs. Families can be diverse in terms of their experience, resources and expectations as well as their cultural, religious and linguistic influences.

▶ Optimum support for a disabled child will only occur when parents are considered to be valued and equal partners alongside the range of professionals working with them and their child.

(DfES, 2003)

The document identified the priorities for service development and the key barriers to effective service delivery and working in partnership with families. It also reported on the factors which had a positive impact on service development and provision and these have been incorporated into the development of the **Early Support** initiative and materials designed to implement 'Together from the Start'.

## Explaining Early Support

The resulting Early Support initiative is a government programme aimed at providing high-quality, coordinated, child- and family-centred services for young children from birth to three, who are disabled or have complex health needs.

Research had shown that a substantial number of families with children with complex health needs or disabilities reported 'a constant battle' to:

▶ find out what services were available;

▶ discover the role of different agencies and professionals;

▶ get professionals to understand their particular situation and needs;

▶ get professionals to recognise their knowledge of their own child;

▶ negotiate delays and bureaucracy.

A major reason for the problems faced by families was identified as the:

> multiplicity of agencies and professionals involved ..., the lack of co-ordination between different agencies and the burden on the family in terms of multiple contacts.' (Sloper et al., 1999)

The Early Support initiative aims to address these issues through developing a service to involve health, education, social services and voluntary sector organisations working in partnership to provide multi-agency support for those children and families.

> The starting point is respect for the daily reality of family life for parents who are raising young children in a situation which presents them with repeated, unusual and unpredictable challenges and which is often highly emotionally charged. Improved service provision means joint decision making, the right information at the right time and enough continuity of support to enable parents to take decisions and initiate positive action to help their child. (DfES, 2004: 18)

A model of support and a range of materials have been developed to implement this initiative. Health or education professionals working with children with complex needs and their families will have access to these materials and together with the family will decide who is to be the key worker or coordinator of the support.

The materials include the following:
**For professionals:**

1 **Professional Guidance** which includes:
   – Talking with families about disability

- Referring on

- Finding out what children and families need

- Sharing information about families

- Making sure families have the information they need

- Key working, key workers and care coordination

- Making and reviewing joint plans

- Monitoring change and development

- Working across boundaries to support families better

- Planning and implementing service improvement.

2 A **Service Audit Tool** with guidance on how to use it.

3 A **Monitoring Protocol for deaf babies and children** with supporting materials.

**For families:**

The **Early Support Family Pack** consisting of:

1. A **Family File** containing

- Introducing ourselves

- List of professionals working with us

- Record of professional contacts

- Family Service Plan

- What our child can do now

- Current records

- Local organisations and contacts.

The **Family Service Plan** is a written plan taking the lead from the family. It is put together after joint discussion with all those involved with the child about the services that the child needs, the current priorities, how the child is developing and how the local services will respond. As a result of these discussions targets may be set and a plan of action made setting out which professionals should do what and when.

Taking the lead in coordinating this plan will be the family's **key worker** or care coordinator. Families can choose their own key worker, though it is usually a professional who has the most regular contact with the family who takes on the role of coordinating services. The family can also choose to coordinate services themselves.

2. **Background Information File**. This contains details of professional roles, information on childcare, financial help, education and statutory assessment, health services, social services, useful contacts and organisations and a glossary of terms.

3. **History File**. This is a file in which to store paperwork no longer in use.

In addition there are **Guides for Parents** on:

- Autistic spectrum disorders

- Cerebral palsy

- Deafness

- Learning disabilities

- Multi-sensory impairment

- Speech and language difficulties

- Visual impairment

- If your child has a rare condition

- When your child has no diagnosis.

## Supporting parents through statutory assessment

The proportion of children with a statement of educational needs remains small even within the group of children with special or additional needs. For those children and families who do go through this process it can be a bewildering and often frustrating experience. For some parents requesting a statutory assessment is a positive part of a journey in which they have tried to gain the support they believe their child needs. For others it is negative process which they undertake reluctantly because they feel it labels and singles out their child as being different.

Practitioners can help parents during this time in the following ways:

- **By having clear, basic information about the process itself**
  Parents want the best for their children and although practitioners and professionals can offer advice it must be the decision of the parents whether or not a request for a statutory assessment is to be made. They can make an informed choice only if they have all the facts and have considered all the options for their child. Parents need to understand the process, how long it takes, what they need to do at each stage and the possible outcomes.

  A useful parent information leaflet 'Let's Talk About … Statutory Assessments and Statements of Educational Need' and a summary chart of the assessment process are included at the end of the chapter.

- **By being clear about their own part in the process**
  The practitioners and professionals working with individual children with special/additional needs will obviously be key in advising and supporting parents at this time. Many will have experience of guiding parents through the process, supplying reports and information based on their own work with the child. Others will be less experienced and need to contact their own support network of advisory teachers, area SENCOs or team managers.

  While they contribute to the process, individual professionals or practitioners have no decision-making role and can influence any possible outcome only through the reports and information they supply. Practitioners and professionals should therefore try to remain impartial and not pre-empt the decision of the local authority.

### ▌ By directing parents to appropriate support services

Every local authority is required to provide a **Parent Partnership Service** which is freely available to all parents of children with special educational needs. Its role is to give independent advice on any aspects of educational provision including requesting a statutory assessment, understanding statements and appealing against local authority decisions. They will help with reading or writing letters or reports and can also support parents at meetings.

Other support services are listed at the end of the book.

# Let's Talk About ...

## Statutory Assessments and Statements of Educational Need

Q. *What is a request for a statutory assessment?*

A. A request for a statutory assessment is when the local authority is asked to carry out a formal assessment of your child in order to decide whether or not they need a statement of educational need. The procedure and timescale for doing this is set out in the Special Educational Needs Code of Practice.

Q. *What is a statement of educational need?*

A. A statement of educational need is a document which describes a child's needs and the support that they should receive. It may also allocate additional resources to help provide that support.

Q. *How do I know if my child needs a statement of educational need?*

A. The practitioners and professionals working with your child will discuss your child's progress with you at each review of their Individual Plan (IP) or Individual Education Plan (IEP). If your child is not making progress despite all possible help being offered by the setting, it may be felt that only additional resources not available from within the setting are needed, and then a request for a statutory assessment may be considered.

Q. *Who can request an assessment?*

A. Parents or early years settings, (with parental support and advice from other professionals) can request a statutory assessment.

Q. *Does the local authority have to assess my child?*

A. Each local authority has criteria for evaluating whether a child needs a statutory assessment or not. It will consider all the evidence that you, the pre-school setting and any other professionals submit against this criteria when making a decision. Generally a child would be experiencing lifelong, complex and significant difficulties and their needs could not be provided for from within the resources normally available to the early years setting.

Q. *Who can help and give me advice about this process?*

A. The practitioners and professionals working with your child can give you information and support. Every local authority also has a Parent Partnership Service which gives independent advice and support to parents of children with special/additional needs. This ranges from general advice, to help with writing letters and support at meetings.

# Statutory Assessment Request Procedures ( 26 weeks)

| Practitioners | Local authority | Parents |
|---|---|---|
| **Request a statutory assessment**<br>This is usually done by using a standard form provided by the local authority.<br><br>Details of all professionals involved with the child should be provided.<br><br>Receive information about a panel date when the request will be considered.<br><br>Respond to a request for any information or reports. This should be sent in by the date given. | **Receive a request for a statutory assessment and acknowledge receipt of this within two weeks.**<br><br>▶ Set a date for 6 weeks ahead when the request will be considered by the local authority panel.<br>▶ Write and ask for any reports or information from the early years setting or school and any education or health professional who they know to be working with the child. These reports will need to be received by the given date.<br><br>**The panel meets, considers all the information against the criteria and decides whether or not the child needs a formal or statutory assessment.** | **Request a statutory assessment**<br><br>This is usually done by writing a letter outlining the reasons for the request.<br><br>▶ Details of all professionals involved with the child should be provided.<br><br>Receive information about a panel date when the request will be considered.<br><br>Respond to a request for any information or reports, including any from private therapists or professionals.<br>This should be sent in by the date given. |
| If the request is turned down you may be asked to attend a meeting with parents and the local authority to discuss the decision and further options. | If the panel decide **not to agree** to the request for a statutory assessment all parties will be informed and parents will be invited to meet and discuss this with the local authority. | If the request is turned down meet with the local authority to discuss the decision and further options. |
| Receive notification of the panel's decision and request for 'advice'.<br><br>The information sent with the original request can be updated or submitted again. New IEPs for example, should be included in the updated setting 'advice'. | If the panel **agree** to the request for statutory assessment:<br>▶ Parents, practitioners and professionals will be asked to submit up-to-date reports and information on the child's needs and progress called 'advice'.<br>▶ Request that this 'advice' should be sent to the local authority within 6 weeks | If the situation is not resolved parents have the right to go to the Independent SEN Tribunal to present a case for an assessment to take place. The Tribunal will make their decision after the meeting.<br><br>Receive notification of the panel's decision and request for 'advice'. |
| It should be returned by the given date. | **Once all the advice has been received the local authority can either:**<br>▶ Decide not to issue a statement because the child's needs can be met without one and issue a '**note in lieu**' instead.<br>or<br>▶ write a **Statement of Educational Need** which outlines the child's needs and levels of support and resources | The information sent with the original request can be updated or submitted again. It is the parents' responsibility to send in reports from any private professionals as part of their parental 'advice'.<br>It should be returned by the given date. |
| Practitioners should contact the local authority representative within 15 days if they disagree with any part of the **draft** statement. | This is sent out as a **draft** to parents and everyone who has contributed advice.<br><br>Within 8 weeks if all are in agreement with the statement and levels of support and resources a **final signed statement** is sent out. | If parents agree with what the **draft** statement says they can ask for a particular setting or school to be named on the statement.<br><br>If parents do not agree with the statement they should indicate this within 15 days and enter into discussion with the local authority representatives. |

Adapted from DfES (2001)

*Working with Parents of Children with Special Educational Needs*, Paul Chapman Publishing © Chris Dukes and Maggie Smith, 2007

**Further reading**

Department for Education and Skills (2001) *Special Educational Needs: A Guide for Parents and Carers*. DfES.

Department for Education and Skills (2003) *Together from the Start – Practical Guidance for Professionals Working with Disabled Children*. DfES.

Department for Education and Skills (2004) *Early Support: Professional Guidance*. DfES.

Department for Education and Skills/Department of Health (2005) *Managing Medicines in Schools and Early Years Settings*. DfES.

Mortimer, H. (2004) *The Essential A to Z Guide to Special Needs: Information on Terms and Conditions, How You Can Help, Where to Go to Find Out More* (Special Needs in the Early Years). Scholastic.

# Contacts and useful organisations

**Chris Dukes and Maggie Smith** (authors of the Hands on Guides)
www.earlymatters.co.uk

**Advice for parents**
www.ace-ed.org.uk

**Afasic (Association for All Speech Impaired Children)**
50–52 Great Sutton Street
London EC1V 0DJ
Tel: 020 7490 9410 Administration
Tel: 0845 355 5577 Helpline
www.afasic.org.uk

**Alliance for Inclusive Education**
Unit 2, 70 South Lambeth Road
London SW8 1RL
www.allfie.org.uk

**British Council of Disabled People**
Litchurch Plaza
Litchurch Lane
Derby DE24 8AA
Tel: 01332 295551
www.bcodp.org.uk

**Cerebral palsy support**
www.scope.org.uk

**Children in Scotland**
5 Shandwick Place
Edinburgh EH3 4RG
Tel: 0131 228 8484
www.childreninscotland.org.uk

**Contact a family**
209–211 City Road
London EC1V 1JN
Tel; 0207 608 8700
www.cafamily.org.uk

**Disabled Living Foundation**
Offers a free advice service on specialist equipment etc.
Tel: 020 7829 6111

**Down's Syndrome Association**
155 Mitcham Road
London SW17 9PG
Tel: 020 8682 4001
www.dsa-uk.com

**IPSEA Tribunal Support Service**
Free advice for parents of children with special educational needs
www.ipsea.org.uk

**MENCAP**
MENCAP works with people with a learning disability and their families and carers
www.mencap.org.uk

**National Association for the Education of Sick Children (NAESC)**
NAESC ensures that all children and young people get the education they need when they are sick
www.sickchildren.org.uk

**National Early Years Network**
77 Holloway Road
London N7 8JZ
Tel: 020 7607 9597

**Netmums**
124 Mildred Avenue
Watford
WD18 7DX
www.netmums.com

**OAASIS (Office for Advice, Assistance, Support and Information on Special Needs)**
Provides a free information and support service for parents, teachers and other professionals
with an interest in special education for children and young adults
www.oaasis.co.uk

**ParentsCentre**
Information and advice for parents, support for children with special education needs, disability, medical needs, and finding support groups.
www.parentscentre.gov.uk

**Parents for Inclusion**
Helping parents so that disabled children can learn, make friends and have a voice in ordinary school and throughout life, a national charity based in London.
Unit 2, 70 South Lambeth Road,
London SW8 1RL
www.parentsforinclusion.org.uk

**The Royal National Institute for the Blind**
www.rnib.org.uk

**Whizz-Kidz**
A national charity aimed at improving independence for children with mobility difficulties
Tel: 0208 7233 600
E-mail: info@whizz-kidz.org.uk

# Government guidance and advice

## England

**SureStart**
www.surestart.gov.uk

**The Early Childhood Unit**
www.earlychildhood.org.uk

**QCA (Qualifications and Curriculum Authority)**
Sets of materials on diversity and inclusion
www.qca.org.uk

## Northern Ireland

**Pre-school guidance**
www.deni.gov.uk/preschool

**Children's services: Northern Ireland**
www.childrensservicesnorthernireland.com

## Scotland

**Children in Scotland**
www.childreninscotland.org.uk

**Learning and Teaching Scotland**
www.ltscotland.org.uk

## Wales

**Children in Wales**
www.childreninwales.org.uk

# References

DfES (2003) *Together from the Start*. London: DfES.

DfES (2004) *Early Support: Professional Guidance*. London: DfES.

Hoffman, M. L. (1987) *Empathy and Its Development*. Cambridge: Cambridge University Press.

Hurt, J. A. (2000) 'Create a parent place: make the invitation for family involvement real', *Young Children*, 55 (5): 88–92.

Moore, C. (1993) 'Maximizing family participation in the team process', in L. Küpper (ed.), *Second National Symposium on Effective Communication for Children and Youth with Severe Disabilities*. McLean, VA: Interstate Research Associates.

Sloper, P. et al. (1999) 'Facilitators and barriers for co-ordinated multi-agency service', *Child Care, Health and Development*, 30 (6): 571–80.

# Index